PRACTICAL HAPJU-KIDO

A PRACTICAL APPLICATION OF AN AMERICAN MARTIAL ART

A Sensible approach for the average person's need to defend themselves

GRANDMASTER
Craig Hutson

Practical HapJu-Kido
A Practical application of an American Martial Art
© 2024 Craig Hutson. Brother Hood of Martial Artists.

No part of this book may be reproduced or transmitted in any form or by any means, electronic or mechanical, including but not limited to: photocopying, recording, or by any information storage retrieval system without the written permission of the publisher, except for the inclusion of brief quotations in a review.

Photography: Mr. Gerade M. Hutson
Cover Design and Interior Layout: Kendra Cagle, 5 Lakes Design

978-1-7360764-3-9 (paperback)
978-1-7360764-4-6 (Kindle)
978-1-7360764-5-3 (ePub)

Library of Congress Control Number: 2024908221

For Additional Information Contact:
Grandmaster Craig Hutson
www.DragonKido.com

TABLE OF CONTENTS

Introduction i
Chapter 1 | Why Should We Learn To Defend Ourselves? 1
Chapter 2 | The Meaning of HapJu-Kido 3
Chapter 3 | Mission Statement 7
Chapter 4 | History of A Street Fighter 9
Chapter 5 | School of Thought 11
Chapter 6 | Essential Virtues 17
Chapter 7 | Power Patterns in Human Attitudes /
                Dan Joon Breathing 21
Chapter 8 | A House Wives Experience with Courage 25
Chapter 9 | Principles Concerning the Nature of Energy 27
Chapter 10 | Fostering Self-Directed Behavior 31
Chapter 11 | Character Qualities / Point of View /
                 What do you stand for? 33
Chapter 12 | The SEVEN VIRTUES OF BUSHIDO 37
Chapter 13 | HAND AS A Defensive Tool 41
     Palm Hand *41*
     Four Knuckle – Traditional Fist *42*
     The Jab and Cross *42*
     The Shovel Hook *43*
     The Uppercut *44*
     Four Knuckle-Flat Hand *44*
     Open Backhand *44*
     Hammer Fist *44*

    Two Finger Tip 45

    Thumb Tip-Jab 46

    Elbow Strike / Forearm Strike 46

    Knife-Hand..47

Chapter 14 | Essential Kicks as a Weapon......................49

    Roundhouse / Turning Kick (Dolly Chagi) 50

    Front Kick / W. Heel 50

    Sidekick (Yup, Chagi) 51

    Inside Crescent Kick (Bandal An Chagi) 51

    Inside Low Angle or Twisting Kick / Inside arch-Slap Kick....51

    Back Kick (Dwi Chagi) 52

    Knee Strike (Moorup Chagi) 52

    Hook Kick/Whip Kick (Dwi Huryeo Chagi)..............53

    Shin Kick...54

    Checking Kick-Lower Area of Execution 54

    Drop Wheel Kick...55

    Cut Kick, Known as a pushing Kick (Mireo-Ahp-Chagi).....55

Chapter 15 | Practical Street Throwing Techniques 57

    Headlock Sweep / Harai Gosh Makikomi 57

    Shoulder Arm Grip..58

    One Arm Shoulder / Ippon-Seoi-Nage......................59

    Circle Sacrifice / Kazuri Tomoe Nage.......................60

    Kibisu-Gaeshi..61

    Outer Sweeping / O-Soto Gari................................61

    Sweeping Leg / Hari-Goshi.....................................62

    Deep Hip Wheel / Koshi Guruma............................64

    Two-Hand Reap / Morote-Gari 65

    Outer Leg Block..65

    Hip Wheel / Koshi-Guruma 66

    Large Outer Reap / Osoto-Gari..68

    Large Outer Drop / Osoto-Otoshi..69

    Outer Wraparound Throw / Makikomi..................................70

Chapter 16 | Joint Bars, Cranks, and Locks.....................................73

    Outward Wrist Lock..73

    Lapel Grab to Elbow Clamp Assist.......................................74

    Tricep Grab...75

    Chicken Hand Goose Neck / Hyper flexing Wrist Lock........76

    Top of Shoulder Grab 77

    Side by Side, Huge..78

    They are in your face...79

    Goose Neck 79

    Four Finger Hold..80

    Two-Hand Palm Press 80

    Boxing Thumb Lock 81

    Outward Wrist Lock..82

Chapter 17 | Striking Points on the Body 85

    General Target Areas...**85**

    Temple / (extremely dangerous) 86

    Bridge of Nose...86

    Ear / Ear Drum 88

    Auricular Nerve Below Ear Drum 88

    Nerve at Upper Lip / Base of Nose.......................................89

    Tip of Jaw / Jaw 89

    Cheek Bone / Chin / Cheek 90
    Adam's Apple Larynx / Extremely Dangerous / Trachea.....91
    Collarbone (clavicle) / next to the trachea 91
    Stomach 92
    Knees – Front, Side, Back, and Shins........................92
    Solar Plexus 93
    Ribs, Thoracic Nerves between Ribs 93
    In Step / Ankle Joint 94
    Hair..95
    Base of Skull..95
    Shoulder and Shoulder Blade 95
    Elbows...97
    Wrists 98
    Fingers 98
    Thighs and Tailbone-Coccyx................................99
    Kidneys...100
    Neck...101
    Back of Knee..101

Chapter 18 | Unorthodox Street Fighting Skills................103
    #1   Deflect /Headlock Take Down........................103
    #2   Elbow Strike 104
    #3   Left Hand Jab...104
    #4   Open Hand Flicker Strike............................105
    #5   Four Knuckle Upper Cut Punch 105
    #6   Knee Strike 105
    #7   Leg Sweep 106
    #8   Low Roundhouse executed with shine 106
    #9   Open Hand Flicker Back Hand......................107

#10	Ear Pop	107
#11	Pelvic Back Kick	108
#12	Leg Grab	108
#13	Forearm Thrust	109
#14	Knee Clip	109
#15	Rear Naked Choke Hold	109
#16	Tuck and Role	110
#17	Solar Plex Strike and Throw	110
#18	Head Lock Wrench	111
#19	Inner Knee Strike	111
#20	Club Kick to Backside	112
#21	Cross-Grip Strike	112
#22	Jugular Stike	112
#23	Index Finger Poke	113
#24	Ridge hand Strike	113
#25	Hooking	114

Chapter 19 | Quick and Dirty..115

    History..117

Chapter 20 | Miscellaneous Tid Bits...........................121

Citations...127

INTRODUCTION

Practical HapJu-Kido gives viewers an in-depth look at the various self-defense techniques taught by this discipline through detailed descriptions. The methods discussed in each chapter are illustrated with a plethora of images. If you want to learn to focus intently and hit your targets with little effort, this book is for you. The importance of being fully present in the here and now is also emphasized. Over the course of fifty years, Master Hutson has established himself as a pivotal figure among martial arts educators. His approach to personal and character development is interesting since it combines aspects of several martial arts forms with tactics for developing one's cognitive processes and character.

Building character prompted him to think of an exciting and valuable solution. Consequently, there is a set of fundamental rules that HapJu-Kido instructors and students should follow. We anticipate that everyone concerned will acquire them and put them to good use. In social situations, one should act by the standards of etiquette, modesty, uprightness, perseverance, self-control, and an unchanging character. The seven deadly sins taught by the world's leading faiths and their association with inherent character attributes should be known by everyone interested in the arts, according to Master Hutson's conclusion. Motivating people to be truthful and morally upright may boost their social standing since it promotes the growth of commendable personal qualities. In this work, Master Hutson defines the meaning of virtue.

Also included is the perspective of Master Hutson. No one who truly practices martial arts would encourage their pupils to violate their moral principles.

The dynamic martial art known as HapJu-Kido combines Judo, Hapkido, Taekwondo, and Street Fighting elements. Its purpose is to provide individuals with the tools they need to become more confident and capable of protecting themselves.

It is upon individuals to develop the character traits necessary for living an authentic life and to learn the essential and valuable skills that can be used for self-defense. It would be best to build self-assurance that meets the requirements. A martial art that teaches aesthetics and self-defense, HapJu-Kido was created to help people. All the essential strategies for improving one's defensive talents are condensed into this work of art from the most authentic, traditional, and perceptive sources. Successful skills have been developed using these methods. Several methods came together to form this work of art. Developing one's sense of self-assurance is the most valuable outcome of training in this art form. Please note that the sport karate methods are most effective when practiced in a structured setting. On the other hand, they are engaged in a street brawl and believe participating in karate tournaments could lead to trouble.

Remember that martial arts training is about more than simply fighting; it's about living life to the fullest.

"I Believe" is a viewpoint I hope all martial artists can embrace. This concept and manner of life should be deeply believed in by all martial artists. I get it; we figured out how to fight. However, we only take action to defend ourselves when doing so is essential and commensurate with the gravity of the offense. We need to develop the qualities that make us fearless and caring.

In the event of an attack, we must constantly be prepared to protect ourselves or others to the same extent.

A more contemporary and practical version of the more conventional Asian fighting styles is the martial art called HapJu-Kido. By fusing traditional combat systems and street fighting techniques, Master Hutson created this unique American martial art.

CHAPTER ONE

"WHY SHOULD WE LEARN TO DEFEND OURSELVES?"

Logic dictates the importance of self-defense. The truth is that you can only sometimes trust people. There are Good, Bad, Conflicted, and Evil People. Keeping this in mind is paramount. However, it is a part of life that we may have thoughts about the other three categories of persons.

Consequently, you will likely have a paltry amount of genuine and trustworthy pals.

- When most people say they are "Good People," it means they are morally conscious. Most people feel terrible about it after committing an immoral or harmful act. To have a conscience is to be aware of a feeling or idea within oneself that causes one's moral compass to determine the appropriateness of an action.

- Bad People have to strive every day to suppress their opposing ideas. They know that their obsession with causing harm to others is excessive. They are unable to maintain self-control.

- Conflicted people are individuals who exist on a spectrum between those who are decent and those who are bad; they are fundamentally dishonest, and they do not care.

- The term "Evil" designates an entirely different entity. Evil individuals believe that it is OK to be terrible. They think it is morally and ethically acceptable and accessible to any reservation.

CHAPTER TWO

THE MEANING OF HAPJU-KIDO

Character Concept's

The traditional tenets of the martial arts principles are Courage, Humility, Integrity, Perseverance, Self-Control, and Indomitable-Spirit.

The creator of HapJu-Kido, Craig Hutson, intuitively translates his personal life experiences into empathy for others. His father was an erratic drinker with a

horrifying near-fatal vehicle accident that almost claimed his and all five children's lives. The pain that Craig experienced due to this incident made the eleven-year-old child vow to be unlike his father. Craig was reared in a troubled, alcoholic household and found it challenging to comprehend the strict and ineffectual parenting that contributed to his sense of helplessness. Craig expressed a lot of his annoyance through street fights. Craig decided to study martial arts as an adult to shape his conception of what it meant to be a mature person. This decision helped him to gain a strong sense of emotional self-control.

The intention behind HapJu-Kido is to combine street fighting elements with the traditional martial arts of **Tae Kwon Do, Hapkido,** and **Judo**. HapJu-Kido is a unique art due to its inclusion of **Boxing skills** along with **Wrestling skills**. Be wary because street fighters are **infamous** for their unconventional tactics.

HapJu-Kido is a blended martial art that heavily incorporates street fighting techniques. Although the concept of **HapJu-Kido** was first conceived in 1976, it was not until 2019 that Grand Master Craig Hutson, the art's founder, was able to establish the style and subsequently create its name in the United States. After that, Grand Master Hutson established a group called "BOMA," or the Brotherhood of Martial Artists.

HapJu-Kido's framework makes it practical, adaptable, and efficient in various situations and conflict intensities. It is no surprise that street fighting is forbidden at regular athletic events. Taekwondo kicks have a great deal of Force, even when thrown from a great distance. Simultaneously, successful close-quarters fighting is made feasible by the throws, locks, chokes, and joint manipulation techniques included in hapkido and judo.

The skills in Street Fighting are such that Master Hutson has been using them for decades to teach the practical ideology of self-defense.

This has been the case because Street Fighting skills are dynamic compared to other disciplines. The meaning behind the name HapJu-Kido is something that most people need to become familiar with. Unfortunately, hearing the words "street fighter" is typically a frightening experience for most people.

CHAPTER THREE

MISSION STATEMENT FOR DRAGON KIDO AUTHENTIC MARTIAL ARTS

The martial arts school known as Dragon Kido Authentic Martial Arts emphasizes staying true to the past. We heavily emphasize the students' growth and development in character and teach them the practical physical talents and techniques common to many martial arts schools. However, we also strive to instill in our students the values and characteristics of acceptance, tranquility, self-control, self-assurance, and respect for oneself and others. We ensure the students will learn a balance of sports, karate, and the value of learning street techniques.

"The intellect has little to do on the road to discovery. There comes a leap in consciousness; call it intuition or what you will, and the solution comes to you, and you do not know how or why. All great discoveries are made in this way."

—ALBERT EINSTEIN

"To have respect for ourselves guides our morals, and deference for others governs our manners."

—LAURENCE STERNE

CHAPTER FOUR

HISTORY OF A STREET FIGHTER

In the annals of street fighting, Craig Hutson stands tall. In his younger years, he had many challenges. Those challenges originated from not being able to walk to school safely. In his domain, he was beset with difficulties. The biggest challenge was living with a sibling and his friends, who were thugs. His brother had friends among the street urchins. It was in their blood to commit crimes. Although his brothers' friends were much bigger and more powerful than Craig's, Craig's father thought it was best for Craig to face his brother's friends alone. After experiencing bullying on multiple occasions, Craig realized that he needed to take the initiative in physical confrontations by striking first. He found it interesting how his brothers would exhibit consistent behavior. Whoever went away was right, regardless of whether what they did on the street was right or wrong. It had nothing to do with ethics or kindness. It was, if not their first thought, then certainly their first impression.

You would likely find yourself in a pool of blood if you refrained from landing the initial blow if you give it any thought.

Is it acceptable to expect to possess specific physical attributes, such as being tall and powerful or having the ability to execute intricate martial arts techniques?

Instead, you need to be familiar with basic tactics for resolving conflicts and improving your mental and physical agility to respond with conviction and speed. Imagine you were given the opportunity to study the topic in advance.

I beg you to prepare yourselves fully for this reality.

HAPJU-KIDO is a modern martial arts form that is especially useful. Please think about What a street fighter searches for before a battle. Our time spent living on the streets gave rise to what is now called HAPJU-KIDO.

These are three time-tested techniques for utilizing "fear" to your advantage. While in the streets, you can confront the three main enemies. The pushers, the verbally abusive person, and the direct assailants are your three enemies if they want to threaten you.

Being "nice" is not the key to quickly defusing heated situations; you must employ techniques to earn respect. Practice the steps until you can recite them aloud to get the feel of them.

CHAPTER FIVE

SCHOOL OF THOUGHT

God created us to answer the questions that pop into our minds. When we stop and think about this, we always answer questions and don't give that fact of ourselves much thought. Hmmm!

We exercised caution during each stage of the production and design process for our Dragon Kido Authentic Martial Arts patch. This item is much more than a simple ornamental accent that can be attached to our dress uniforms; it is an essential component of those uniforms. In addition to that, it serves a vital functional purpose. The members of our Academy are strongly encouraged to study the guiding principles portrayed in this official emblem to learn the essential life skills our school strives to assist each student in acquiring. Our school seeks to help each student in achieving these skills. We see it in that light since it is so much more than a simple cosmetic element that will be attached to our dress clothes. It is strongly advised that every member of the Academy studies the guiding principles reflected in this official insignia to acquire a more exceptional knowledge of the fundamental life skills that our Academy's job is to assist each student in learning. Our Academy's duty is to help each student acquire these skills. In addition to this, Kido the Dragon encircles the triple-tiered synergy swirl that serves as our Academy's "Character to the Core" insignia. This logo represents the past, the present, and the future.

What is vital to the school is that the individuals understand that forming one's character is a continuing process that positively impacts the individual, the community, and the world. The background of our school emblem, which is tricolored and consists of red, blue, and gold, also reflects the mental, physical, and spiritual components of martial arts training and the necessity of finding balance in one's life. The colors red, blue, and gold are in the same proportions as the three primary colors of our school insignia. In the mythology and folklore of many Asian nations, a dragon is a symbol of heaven. This indicates that those practicing Dragon Kido should strive toward lofty goals, such as aiming to acquire martial arts excellence, which must include freely offering service to others.

Our Martial Arts Academy is a proud member of the Martial Artists' Brotherhood, established through the collaboration of Grandmaster Hutson and Black Belt Masters worldwide. The BOMA Patch is described in greater detail in the following summary.

The four fingers on the left palm represent the four nourishing components: excellence, health, wisdom, and virtue. These aspects embrace the overall spirit of martial arts as a global practice. The left thumb is positioned in such a way as to give the impression that one should never be proud or self-centered.

On the other hand, the right hand denotes consistent, laborious practice. It is clenched in a fist to signify aggression. At the same time, the left, which represents righteousness and discipline, restricts it. Hence, there is a sense of equilibrium between the two.

The image of yin and yang displayed in the background gives the impression that the yin and yang forces do not compete with one another but rather complement one another. They come together to produce an interactive system in which the total is greater than the sum of its individual components. Similarly, practitioners of various styles unite to build long-lasting alliances, ultimately forming a brotherhood of martial artists. Honesty, bravery, compassion, generosity, faithfulness, Integrity, Justice, self-control, and prudence are some values reflected in Dragon Kido A.M.A.

What Does "The Whole is Greater Than The Sum of Its Parts" Mean?

To wrap up the discussion of our school's character ideals, I must define character in its purest form. Thus, the concept is that the whole is greater than the sum of its parts. One thing will be more equitable, attractive, or ideal when categorized by various elements and qualities than if each aspect were considered separately. The adage "The whole is larger than the sum of its parts" refers to this.

It implies that specific structures and other elements ought to be enhanced.

We must work on it when we know we lack some aspects of our lives. Character is complicated but can be fun to work on. It is forever changing.

Many words we use are conscious and unconscious reflexes based on our belief systems.

"Life is not about being better than someone else but about becoming the best version of yourself."

—MATTHEW KELLY

"I believe martial arts students should acknowledge that martial arts are not just about fighting but about how one lives."

—MASTER HUTSON

"Adapt what is useful, reject what is useless, and add what is specifically your own."

—BRUCE LEE

The above caption is a school of thinking; I aspire to achieve harmony between my physical, mental, and spiritual selves so that I can practice art, reflect on it, and adopt its guiding principles and values. Grasp the fact that, "Yes," we hone our fighting skills. However, we only learn to fight to the extent that we are good fighters; we should also be proportionately nice and have many other admirable attributes.

Value of deep breathing called Dan-Jun

Dan-Jun breathing is easily an essential part of our martial arts experience.

By understanding, developing, and practicing Dan-Jun's breathing, the following will be created:

Maintaining regular, deliberate breathing patterns calls for undivided attention. Focusing on one task at a time improves efficiency, speed, and coordination across the board.

Time and practice are required to acquire proper breathing techniques, so you'll need patience. Being patient is a skill that may be honed through practicing slow, focused belly movements.

The Circulation of Blood by Dan Jun Practicing deep breathing techniques can temporarily enhance blood flow, aiding detoxification and general circulation.

For our internal strength, we consider the Dan-Jun area. Mastering this energy and learning to channel it effectively will grant you superhuman strength and power.

Proper breathing techniques can enhance physical strength and mental fortitude. To begin, returning to your original condition is facilitated by appropriate breathing. We weren't meant to be uncoordinated, slouched, or ill-posed in any way. Moving, standing, running, bending, breathing deeply, and being forceful were all parts of our original design. Going back to your original state will give you more incredible energy.

In addition, you'll be able to coordinate your breathing with your body, enhancing the results. Rigid, connected, and braced bodies are stronger and more capable. Developing this skill is the goal of Dan-Jun's breathing and "dynamic tension" exercises. Rigidity, on the other hand, slows you down. Mastering deep breathing exercises also helps one to unwind physically. Learning to relax while keeping your muscles taut to perform at your best would be best.

CHAPTER SIX

ESSENTIAL VIRTUES

"Parents can only give good advice or put their children on the right path. The final forming of a person's character lies in their own hands."

—ANNE FRANK

Mind, body, and spiritual habits make up a person's virtues. Therefore, it demands consistent work to cultivate the habit of integrity as a way of life. I suspect that most knowledgeable people would say that putting one's principles and values into practice is ethical behavior.

Wisdom is a condensed form of "knowledge" that uses **COMMON SENSE**. Having insight enables us to judge correctly, recognize what is essential in life, and determine our priorities.

Secondly, Justice means acknowledging and respecting the rights of each person as an individual. Understanding that Justice encompasses self-respect, valuing human rights, and treating everyone with dignity.

Fortitude is the **third attribute.** When confronted with the challenges that life throws us, fortitude is the armor that enables us to continue doing what is right. The inner resiliency that allows us to persevere in the face of adversity and endure physical or emotional suffering is known as fortitude.

The **Fourth** virtue is **Self-control. Self-control** is the governor of our temper, passions, and sexual appetites.

The **Fifth** essential virtue is **Love.** Love is the willingness to sacrifice for the sake of another. To go beyond what the person or institution probably deserves.

The **Sixth** essential virtue is having a **Positive Attitude.** You are a burden to yourself and others with a negative attitude. If you have a positive attitude, you're an asset to yourself and others.

Old-fashioned hard work is a **Seventh** indispensable virtue. There is no substitute in life for work. I challenge you to achieve anything worthwhile without hard work. The ingredients of hard work are initiative, diligence, goal-setting, and resourcefulness.

The **Eighth** essential virtue is **integrity.** Integrity is adhering to moral principles, being faithful to an ethical code, having a conscience surrounding us, and keeping our word. **Integrity is different from honesty, which is telling the truth to people. Integrity is telling the truth to ourselves. Self-deception enables us to do whatever we wish and find a reason to justify our actions.**

Gratitude is the **Ninth** virtue. Gratitude, like Love, is not a feeling but an act of our will.

Humility, the final tenth essential virtue, can be considered the foundation of our moral life. Humility is necessary for acquiring the other virtues. It helps us to be aware of our imperfections.

Humility is recognizing our inadequacies and abilities and pressing our capabilities into service without attracting attention or expecting applause. **An ordinary character flaw in people is the overwhelming attraction to being right.**

Along with the values of the ten virtues, we need to take at the seven deadly sins: **Pride, Envy, Greed, Lust, Anger, Gluttony, and Sloth.**

An intricate Christian concept of sin was passed down to the medieval and early Renaissance periods. There are more than a dozen similar models. The most often used one enumerates seven crimes, breaking them into four corporeal and three spiritual transgressions.

While there was no doubt that all seven sins were terrible crimes that may lead to damnation, most people agreed that spiritual sins were more deadly than sins that sprang only from physical frailty.

We are built to respond to inquiries and reinvent ourselves.

Which virtue is the greatest? Why is it so excellent? Does the philosophy of Aristotle make sense?

Aristotle addresses moral and intellectual qualities in his Nicomachean Ethics. He contends that intelligence is the one attribute that transcends all others. Since it's an end in and of itself, unlike other virtues, it's the finest path to happiness, which is the ultimate objective of life.

CHAPTER SEVEN

POWER PATTERNS IN HUMAN ATTITUDES

Being able to differentiate between higher and lower energy is the first step in becoming mature and realizing that you have the power to shape and change who you are. Realizing that God has given you all you need to make the required changes requires reading about and understanding the power of altering human attitudes and values. The author of the book Power vs. Force is David R. Hawking, M.D., Ph.D.

I quietly spent some time reviewing the terms listed on pages 150 and 151. Dr. Hawkins's study indicates that these phrases help alter our behavior and perceptions. It's a compelling work that anybody interested in changing things should read. As I talk about healthy terms you should use in your life, let me illustrate with a few examples from Dr. Hawkin's book. Please remember that there are 136 distinct pairings on the list in Dr. Hawkin's book. Here are only five instances of what I mean when I say there are both excellent and terrible contrasts in what I am talking about.

Positive ... Negative

Agreeable ... Condescending

Being ... Having

Choosing to ... Having to

Empathetic ... Pitying

Flexible ... Rigid

Global ... Local

Healing ... Irritating

Inspired ... Mundane

Modest ... Haughty

Give this list of recommendations some serious thought and continue researching Dr. Hawking's book. You will discover that the list will assist you in becoming a more improved version of yourself. You will ultimately be able to create the shift to becoming a different person with the assistance of other lists of a similar sort and by putting into practice the healthy left side of this list. The fundamental truth is that anyone who devotes a healthy or fair amount of time to these lists will eventually develop more maturity and character.

"Many words we use are unconscious reflexes based on our belief system. Which we obtained early in life."

However, knowing our words can reveal much about who we are, mainly if people understand what aspects of themselves need improvement.

Consequently, our primary objective is to pursue wholesome descriptive patterns. Words are examples of power patterns because they can connect us to our positive energy and flow, facilitating a connection with our higher selves. When we are more in tune with our higher selves, practice staying healthy, and are aware of our feelings, we become connected to the source of our spirituality, which in turn gives us the ability to practice **Heroic Courage.**

CHAPTER EIGHT

A HOUSEWIVES EXPERIENCE WITH COURAGE

An unexpected event forces a woman to abandon the idea that she is always safe when others are around. Exiting the supermarket, she spots a shadowy figure coming up behind her while walking toward her vehicle. Like a gathering cloud, something ominous was enveloping her. A great wave of excitement washed over her as she stared at a person approaching. She became more aware as the shadow approached, drawing nearer by the second. As the other person was about to seize her, she swiftly turned around. She successfully defended herself from the attack since her reaction caught her attacker off guard. The attacker was thwarted by her usage of a Kobaton key chain. In the heat of battle, she struck her assailant in the ribs with a kobaton blow. In agony, he let out a cry. Her assailant was clearly in agony; he was lying on the ground. Therefore, she managed to get away as soon as she noticed he appeared to be losing the fight. She retrieved her phone, secured her vehicle, and snapped a picture of her assailant in a flash. Upon realizing that she was photographing him, he quickly fled. Thankfully, the self-defense items on her key chain came in handy. A copy of the assailant's picture was then given to the authorities, and she contacted them by phone after the incident.

History

A kubotan is a keychain weapon developed by Takayuki Kubota in the late Sixties based on the Hashi stick, an invention of his father. It's usually no longer than 5 1/2" and about a 1/2" in diameter.

Important Note:
Check with your state's legality before purchasing a Kubatan.

CHAPTER NINE

PRINCIPLES CONCERNING THE NATURE OF ENERGY

Fight, Flight, Flow, Water, Circular, and Sum are frequently associated with this type of martial art. The following will concisely explain these ideas and how they might be understood and relate to one another.

The Fight Principle

There is no way to escape the inextricable connection between the Fight principle and fleeing or putting up a fight. Alterations in the Nervous System and the Secretion of a Powerful Hormone Called (Epinephrine, Also Known as Adrenaline) are Part of the Sequence of Activities that Occur Within the Body When It Gets Ready to Fight or Flee for Safety.

When the body is getting ready to fight or flee for safety, it goes through a series of activities that prepare it to fight or flee. A critical point to make here is that we actually are calling on our primitive and primal selves. We are very capable of momentary, vicious, defensive behavior.

What most people are afraid of is that the person attacking them is doing so in a **vicious manner.**

The Water principle

The Water principle, when practiced, will experience less anxiety if you learn to flow with the situation rather than fighting against it. A practitioner of HapJu-Kido will divert the Force of an attacker who is attacking linearly by guiding the attack in a circular pattern instead. As a result, the incident ends up being beneficial to the student or the person who is deflecting the attack since it adds the **attacker's power to the student's defense.**

The Circular principle

In the Circular principle of HapJu-Kido, the circle emphasizes the redirection of Force and the control of the attacker. It is comparable to Judo and Hapkido and is excellent for developing your fighting skills for the street. Moving in a circular motion makes your attacks more powerful and unpredictable. For instance, predicting the end point of a circle is more complex than predicting the end point of a straight line. On the other hand, circles are far more approachable than different shapes, such as straight lines. We can incorporate various ideas when we accept the circular or spiral thinking concept. Eventually, we will end up at the same point, taking different paths. However, we may still arrive at the same destination.

The Sum Principle

The Sum Principle is a combination of the Water Principle and the Circular Principle, sometimes known as the "sum" of the Water Principle and the Circular Principle. The sum principle is a natural expression of night and day, hot and cold, or happy and sad states of being. They are not mutually exclusive, as each is a self-contained and independent principle. On the other hand, from a philosophical standpoint, how yin and yang interact determines the fate of living things, including people.

CHAPTER TEN

FOSTERING SELF-DIRECTED BEHAVIOR

Great students come in all shapes and sizes. Whether observing classes in the academic world or out on the mat, what sets them apart is not their mental abilities, or even their physical skills, but rather their inner drive.

Independent action is the key to success. Individuals who regularly take charge of their own training and consistently put forth their best efforts, attain excellence. Top students understand the importance of repetition and review their studies willingly. For them, outside recognition is often downplayed because they compete with themselves. High-achievers know how to harness the power of curiosity to fight boredom by delving into subjects deeper. Ordinary life transforms into an exciting adventure.

By contrast, in today's culture, it is not uncommon for people to do only what is necessary to get by--at school and on the job. But so much potential is lost with this limiting perspective. How does one demonstrate initiative and reap the rewards of self-directed behavior?

Be proactive about the learning process. Practice on your own without being told to do so. Focus on the journey, not just the end result. Don't look to others for motivation, but show your commitment and challenge yourself to become better than you were yesterday.

by: Barbara Harville

CHAPTER ELEVEN

CHARACTER QUALITIES/ POINTS OF VIEW / WHAT DO YOU STAND FOR?

Character is the inner values that determine your outer actions.

"You can easily judge a man's character by how he treats those who can do nothing for him."

—MALCOLM S. FORBES

The crucial issue of "What do I stand for?" is posed to the reader in Chapter Five. The question, "Who are you when no one is looking?" comes to mind. Do you act as a leader or a follower? The terms on the list below have definitions, and as a martial artist, they are crucial to incorporate into our way of thinking and feeling about life. You will see a strong feeling of self in yourself when you have a strong sense of principles and have integrated them into your life.

I am only utilizing a handful of the over thirty terms I started with that pertain to character attributes. I didn't want to overdo the character development process; therefore, I decided not to do as many.

You must realize that when it comes time to protect yourself, you don't want to indulge or overthink your morally justified right to self-defense. Most of the time, we have to take quick action. In other words, it's OK to respond from your instincts. That idea might save your life and, most likely, your physical well-being.

Here are a few attributes I have chosen to nurture in myself, which allowed me the added edge I needed to respond in a way that protected me from harm.

Alertness:

You should dedicate a room in your house to practicing the methods for twenty minutes three times a week. Your interest in learning how to develop a natural awareness level is a critical step in developing the character needed to have the drive to protect yourself. Giving someone your whole attention shows attentiveness and demonstrates your value to them.

Faith:

What Is It? Everybody's definition of faith is unique. You would probably receive many responses if you polled one hundred different people. It has a nuanced connotation when addressing faith within a religious setting. Believers have faith.

Confidence:

What is It? When someone is urged to take a risk they don't fully comprehend but manage to take, it boosts their confidence.

Determination and Decisiveness:

Determination and Decisiveness are essential. Great achievers have all succeeded where they are now because of their diligence, devotion, and willpower. The hardest thing in life is not something you can finish in the morning, but you can choose to work at it. Everything starts as a work in progress, but it eventually becomes an accomplishment with enough perseverance.

Initiative:

Initiative, in a few words, is the initial step in a sequence of acts is an initiative. An initiative also refers to a character trait that demonstrates a readiness to accept accountability and complete tasks. An initiative is a beginning that is intended to be continued.

Self-control:

Abstaining from improper action and acting morally. Impulses can manifest as ideas, feelings, or actions. **Self-discipline or self-restraint can be used interchangeably** with the meaning of **Self-control.** Exercising self-control is resisting the urge to act on impulses and choosing the right action when faced with temptation.

To end with the ideas of character or inner values, here are the other traits I mentioned.

(Benevolence, Boldness, Cautiousness, Compassion, Contentment, Creativity, Decisiveness, Deference, Dependability, Determination, Discretion, Endurance, Enthusiasm, Flexibility, Forgiveness, Generosity, Gentleness, Humility, Joyfulness, Justice, Security, Sensitivity, Virtue, and Wisdom.)

Faith, Honor, Humility, Sincerity:

Understanding the significance of being open and honest in one's actions and a desire to act according to genuine and sincere motives is essential.

Tolerance:

Tolerance is the absence of discrimination and the adoption of an impartial and fair attitude toward people whose beliefs, practices, races, faiths, nations, or other characteristics differ from one's own. Tolerance is also the absence of bigotry. Freedom from discrimination is synonymous with freedom from bias.

The book *The Four Agreements* was written by **Don Miguel Ruiz**. My experience with reading Don's book multiple times has taught me the importance of keeping my word to other people. The phrase "I promise" is never used by me. Because of the significance of Don's effort, I have included all four of his agreements. I strongly encourage you to obtain his book and grow in the spirit of character development.

1. "Always be impeccable with your word and speak with integrity. Say Nothing more than what you intend.

2. "Don't Take Anything Personally" (advice to not do so). Nothing that other people do can be traced back to you.

3. Warning: Don't Jump to Conclusions Find the strength to voice your concerns.

4. "You should always try your best." Your best effort is going to evolve from one moment to the next.

CHAPTER TWELVE

THE SEVEN VIRTUES OF BUSHIDO

Integrity (GI)

"True Martial Artists make a full commitment to their decisions."

Be sincerely Honest in your Dealings with all people. Believe in Justice from within yourself.

Respect Polite Courtesy (REI)

"The true martial artist's true strength becomes apparent during difficult times."

True Martial Artists desire not to be cruel. They do not need to demonstrate their power. **True Martial Artists** are courteous even to their enemies. **True Martial Artists** are respected for their strength in confrontation and compassion for their dealings with others. The true power of a **Martial Artist** becomes apparent during difficult times.

Heroic Courage (YUKI)

"Heroic Courage is not blind. It is intelligent and strong."

Rise above the masses of people who are afraid to act. **True Martial Artists** must have Heroic Courage. It is Risky. It is Dangerous. It is living life completely, fully, and thoroughly. Heroic Courage is Intelligent and Strong.

Honor (MEIYO)

"You cannot hide from yourself."

A **True Martial Artist** has only one Judge, "Character." The decisions you make and how these decisions are carried out reflect who you are.

Compassion (JIN)

"If an opportunity doesn't arise, they go out of their way to find one."

The **True Martial Artist** becomes quick and decisive through intense training and hard work.

Honesty and Sincerity (MAKOTO)

"Speaking and doing are the same action."

When **True Martial Artists** say they will act, it is as good as done.

Duty and Loyalty (CHUGI)

True martial artists are responsible for everything they have said and are immensely loyal to all those in their care.

CHAPTER THIRTEEN

HAND AS A DEFENSIVE TOOL

Palm Hand

Bring your palms up in front of your chest as you interact with your attacker; open palms indicate passivity to your attacker.

When striking, you will want to keep your fingers pointed up, and your hand flexed backward. You can create the most power with a steady footing by rotating your hips into the strike.

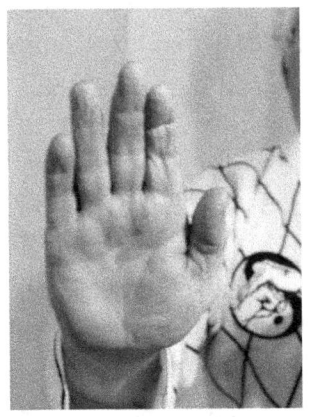

Four Knuckle – Traditional Fist

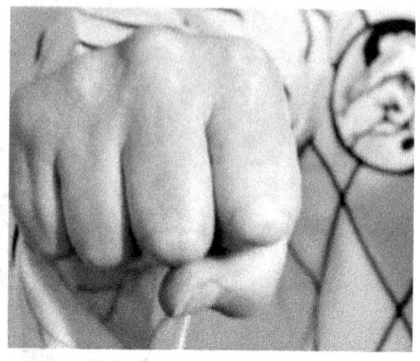

The jab is a punch delivered in a direct line, often from a distance, with the arm positioned above the lead foot. The punch is lightning-fast and packed with Force. This blow must be delivered with the knuckles of the hand rather than a closed fist. Its primary functions are to divert attention, maintain distance, establish a position, and aid in defensive maneuvers.

The Jab and Cross

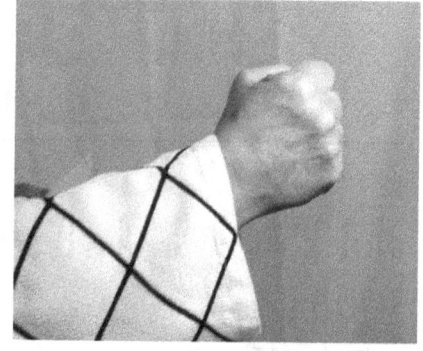

The jab often precedes the cross. Known as a 'jab-cross' or a 'one-two,' this is the most basic and effective combination; the jab is used to get the opponent to react, and the cross shoots straight through into your opponent.

The rear hand is thrown from the chin from the guard position, traveling towards the target in a straight line. The back shoulder comes forward and finishes touching the outside of the chin.

When performing the cover, it is possible to retract the lead hand and tuck it under the face to protect the underside of the chin. When throwing a straight or cross, the torso,y, and hips should twist counterclockwise for dominant right-hand throwers or clockwise for dominant left-hand throwers to provide additional power to the motion. Because the weight is also being moved from the back foot to the front foot, the back heel will shift outwards to facilitate this weight transfer. The Force of the straight-cross move comes from the body rotation and the quick weight transfer.

If the opponent throws the instant, they lead with the same side hand. The name of the blow comes from the fact that it goes across the leading arm. If, on the other hand, the rear hand goes inside the guard of the opponent, then the technique is straight.

It is frequently employed in the process of establishing a hook. Following up a jab with a straight cross can create the essential one-two combination.

The Shovel Hook

You can either throw the hook with your knuckles facing upwards or outwards. These are the two primary methods to do it. Both have advantages and disadvantages, with the primary difference being the street fights' preference for one technique over the other.

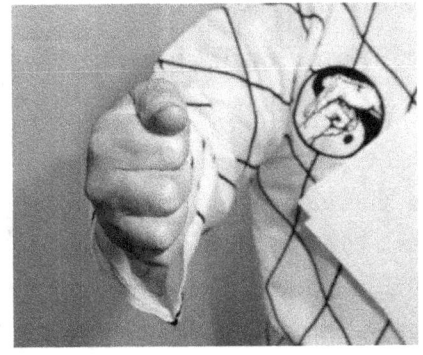

A sizeable fraction of competitors utilize both hooks in their fighting style for various reasons. A shovel hook is a strike delivered at close range and **falls between a hook and an uppercut.** Shovel hooks are most frequently applied at a 45-degree angle to the targeted body part.

For instance, a liver shot can be performed with the assistance of a shovel hook. It is imperative that this blow be delivered with the knuckles of the hand rather than with a closed fist. Because of the weight and momentum that goes into it, the shovel hook is a punch that carries great potential for both risk and profit.

The Shovel Hook can also be executed with the Four Knuckle / Flat Hand. *(See next page)*

The Uppercut

The Uppercut is a punch thrown upward, usually from close range. The power from an uppercut is generated from the legs and is then transferred to the upper body.

The Uppercut can also be executed with the Four Knuckle / Flat Hand.

Four Knuckle / Flat Hand

A four-knuckle strike is a punching technique similar to a high punch. However, the four knuckles of the fingers are extended outward and used to deliver the blow rather than the palm being used as the striking surface. It is the first knuckles that bend to grip something.

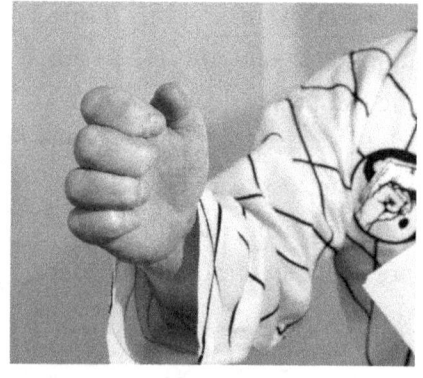

Open Back Hand

Your striking area, index, and middle finger joints are in the square-shaped region on the palm side of your hand.

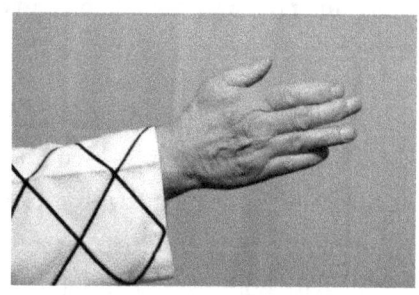

Hammer Fist

The hammer fist is a strike performed with the bottom of a clenched fist, utilizing an action similar to swinging a hammer. However, the hammer fist can also be used horizontally, much like a back fist attack that utilizes the bottom fist.

Because there is no compression of the knuckles or metacarpals and no leverage to bend the wrist, this blow will not cause any injury to the bones in the hands.

It is beneficial for striking the temples, the nose, the jaw, the wrist for blocking punches, the testicles, the sternum, and the ear, although a cupped hand is more effective. The hammer fist impacts places on the body about the size of a cricket ball. 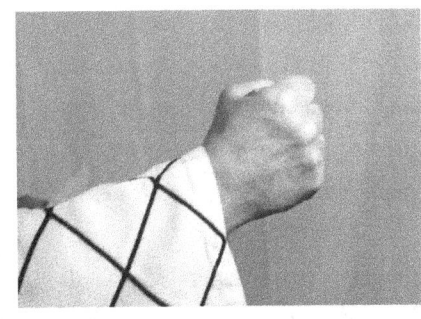 When engaging in "ground-and-pound" hitting in mixed martial arts, practitioners will occasionally use the hammer fist to protect the bones of the hand.

In addition, the hammer fist can be used to defend against grapple charges, in which the attacker goes low, clutches the defender's knees, and hits the back of the defender's head with a blow that causes a concussion. It is a safer option to perform a karate chop on the neck of the attacker, which might potentially be fatal.

Two Finger Tip

The practitioner of this method will begin by bending the thumb, the pinky, and the ring finger of the hand before continuing with the application of this method. After that, you should construct bridge support by crisscrossing your middle 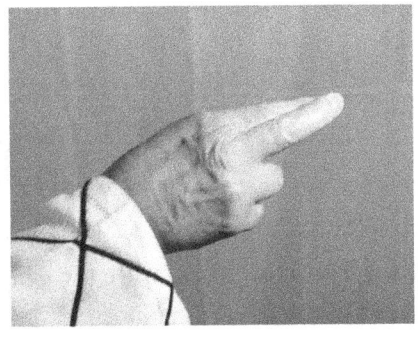 finger over your index finger on the same hand. It is advantageous because you know where to launch the assault on the target. Those targets are the temple, the nose, the jawline, the sternum, the ear, and the side of the nose.

Thumb Tip

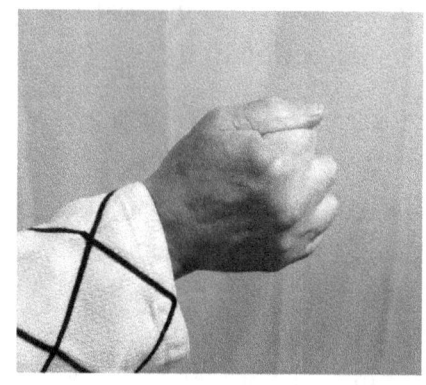

It is possible to perform hand blows with the knuckles extended rather than the conventional fist configuration to deliver a standard punch. The forward movement of one of the fingers allows the knuckle to make contact with the target, thereby focusing the applied Force over a more condensed region. This particular strike style is best suited for attacks that **target pressure points.** These strikes, rooted in traditional martial arts, are not a standard technique because of the precision and conditioning needed comparable to the knuckles for traditional punching. Instead, it is considered a circumstantial technique.

This technique is delivered to the back of the hand while the individual is held against their will. It does this by applying pressure on the smaller bones in the opponent's hand, which causes the opponent's grasp to weaken. This enables a smooth transition for the practitioner into a technique involving the manipulation of tiny joints. Evidence is difficult to collect due to the nature of the art and the fact that it is not used in regular sports. However, its usefulness is more critical during a street fight situation.

Elbow strike / Forearm Strike

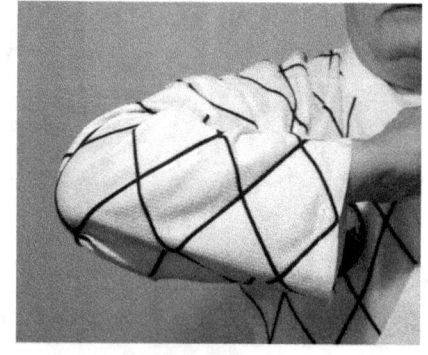

An elbow strike and Forearm Strike are commonly called simply an elbow technique. This technique is a strike with the point of the elbow, the forearm part nearest to the elbow, or the upper part of the upper arm closest to the elbow.

Elbows and forearms can be thrown sideways, upwards, downwards, and most effectively diagonally or indirectly, as well as in several other ways, like during a jump.

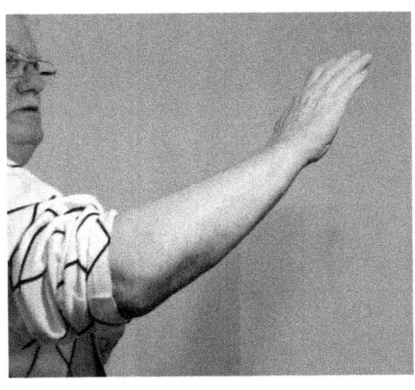

However, elbowing the head increases the risk of lacerations in a fight.

Elbows are not allowed in most modern combat sports; however, when it comes to a self-defense situation, they are permitted. For our purpose as a street fight, this technique is exceptionally effective in stopping an aggressive person.

Knife-Hand Strike or Block

The term "karate chop," the English equivalent of the Japanese word "shut-uchi," is well-known. It describes a hit made with the hand's side opposite the thumb, from the little finger to the wrist. A "knife-hand strike" is the name given to this kind of blow in martial

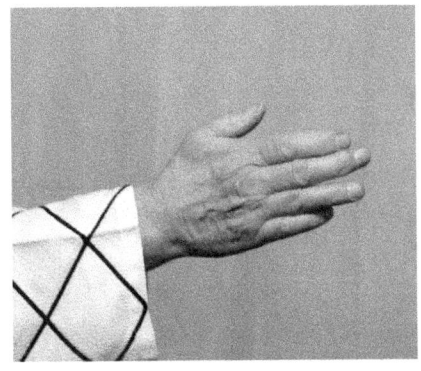

arts. The neck's mastoid muscles, the throat, the collarbones, the ribs, the jaw, the upper arm, the wrist, and the kneecap are all suitable targets for the knife-hand strike. These injuries can render the victim unconscious.

CHAPTER FOURTEEN

ESSENTIAL KICKS AS A WEAPON

Differences in How Organizations Teach Kicks

Honestly, all the influential martial arts organizations teach similar kicks. However, introducing the kicks is a bit different between organizations. For example, BOMA is known for its blended style of teaching self-defense. Similarly, ITF, ATA, AKF, and WTF are geared more toward teaching kicks for tournaments.

The rules of competition a school participates in usually dictate how they teach students kicking skills. For example, competitors like complete contact and point sparring have different kicking rules and kicks they allow.

Roundhouse/Turning Kick (Dollyo Chagi)

A Roundhouse is a typical martial arts kick with variations. To execute this kick, turn your foot (opposite the kicking foot), bring your knee up for height, and turn to bring the kick across your body. It is possible to throw the kick with the other foot.

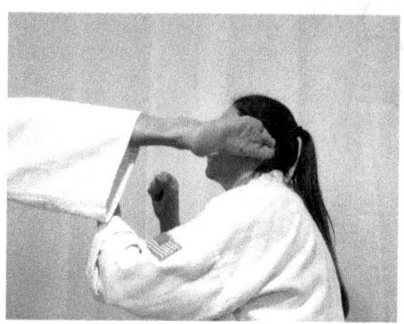 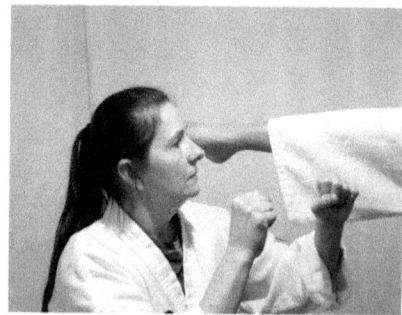

Front Kick / W. Heel

The front kick in martial arts is executed by lifting the knee straight forward, keeping the foot and shin either hanging freely or pulled to the hip, straightening the leg in front of the practitioner, and striking the target area. Retracting the leg immediately after delivering the kick is desirable to avoid the opponent trying to grapple the leg and (unless a combination is in the process) returning to a stable fighting stance.

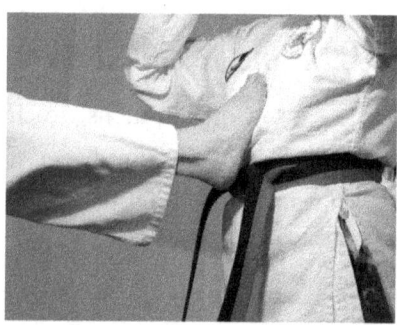 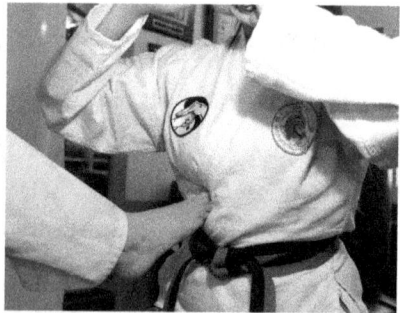

Sidekick (Yup, Chagi)

This kick is slower than most others but powerful when thrown correctly. You're standing sideways and chamber the leg by bringing your knee up to your midsection. The sidekick is usually executed with the foot horizontal and the heel focused on the solar plexus.

Inside Crescent Kick (Bandal Ahn Chagi)

It is similar to an ax kick's motion, and you land with the heel, but you kick with the front leg. Then, you step forward with your back leg and execute the kick from an in-to-out motion.

Two main techniques can be utilized when doing the Crescent Kick. One of these moves is the Arc Kick, which is also referred to as the Bandal Chagi. One kick with a shifting motion is carried out from the inside out toward the outside. The kicking leg is bent in the same manner as it would be for a Front Kick first, and then the knee is aimed in the direction of a target that is either to the left or right of the actual target. The Force generated by the snap is then redirected, which causes the leg to be whipped into an arc and contact the target from the side. Bandal Chagi enables you to go inside their defenses and strike the side of the head or knock down their hands in preparation for a close strike, which you can follow up with. It is effective for getting inside their defenses.

Back Kick (Dwi Chagi)

A backkick is a forceful kick. In this kick, you will use your back leg and turn to the right by 180 degrees to increase your power and speed. You kick with the heel of your foot and aim for the opponent's abdomen or pelvis most of the time; whether or not you can throw a back-kick to the opponent's face depends on the regulations of the competition or your flexibility.

Knee Strike (Moorup Chigi)

Chigi is the correct term to use in place of Chagi when referring to a knee strike because, technically speaking, a knee strike is not a kick. Chigi is the acceptable term. In the context of competitions, it is never allowed. Therefore, the only possible application for it is self-defense. The pushing kick is analogous to a front kick; however, the kicker is propelled forward rather than making contact with the target in a snapping motion. It is a common tactic in defense kicking to employ kicks that drive an opponent away from you to create space.

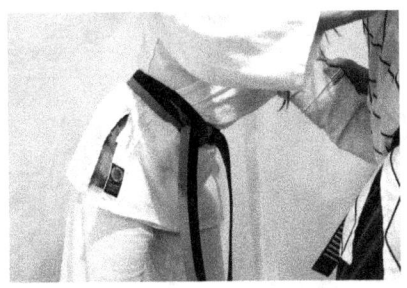 

Hook Kick / Whip Kick (Dwi Huryeo Chagi)

It is very similar to how a sidekick is performed when it comes to how a front hook kick is started. The knee that will be used to kick is brought up to point in the direction of the target first. Then, the foot that will not be used to kick is pivoted to the side after the knee that will be used to kick has been brought up to point in the direction of the target. Because of this, the hip of the leg being kicked rotates counterclockwise due to the kick. On the other hand, the kick used to produce a hook is directed on purpose toward the toes of the kicking foot, which are placed some distance past the target. This is done to perform the hook to catch the target's attention. After this, the leg is stretched to the side of the target to make it possible to strike it with the heel of the foot, which maximizes the effectiveness of the technique. Following that, a blow is delivered to the target. The foot suddenly snaps to the side when the knee is fully extended. Whether or not the kick is successful will be determined by whether part of the foot makes contact with the target (the toe or the heel).

Shin Kick

Shin kicks are a technique that can be useful in street fights because they are excellent at inflicting misery and having a low possibility of injury to the kicker. Shin kicks effectively maintain a safe distance from an attacker, making them a potentially helpful tactic in street battles. Shin kicks can be used to keep an opponent at a safe distance. The most effective form of self-defense is continuously kicking  an attacker in the leg until they feel frustrated. This should continue until the aggressor is defeated. This straightforward method involves minimal physical exertion and may be executed comparatively shortly.

Checking Kick – Lower area of execution

Carrying out a move known as the "Checking Kick" is a very efficient way to ward off an aggressor. For example, to protect your shin or thigh, your leg is lifted and bent at the knee in this position. Similarly, the easiest way to avoid the lower shin or ankle of the attacker is to place your forward foot against it.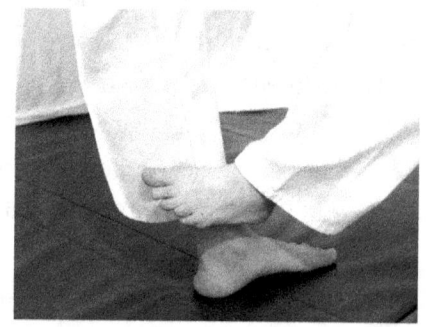

Drop-Wheel Kick

When performing a drop-wheel kick, each of the many distinct martial arts styles has its one-of-a-kind approach to follow. For instance, in Hapkido, the kick is performed by first simulating a movement away from an opponent and then lowering oneself to either the left or right knee, with the left knee deployed in this particular picture. Another example would be the use of the right knee in Judo. Alternately, the kick can be carried out by lowering oneself to one's right knee rather than one's left. After that, you should conduct a wheel kick with your leg straight, aiming to clip the front leg of your opponent while simultaneously spinning your body 180 degrees counterclockwise. While you are doing this, make sure that your other leg is completely straight. Your opponent will almost certainly become unbalanced or fall to the ground. As a result, they are allowing you to finish off the attack with subsequent actions. In the vast majority of situations, the knee or ankle of the aggressor is designed to take the blow from the blow.

Cut Kick, Known as a pushing Kick (Mireo-Ahp-Chagi)

Generally, this technique is often called the front thrust kick or push kick. Use the push kick to create space for yourself, or throw an attacker off their balance. As a result of its ability to halt an opponent's forward momentum or counteract a front kick, the push kick is an effective defensive kick. When defending against a front kick, defenders must be quick on their feet. It requires the defender to perform a pushing kick, which is analogous to the checking kick discussed on the two pages before this one.

CHAPTER FIFTEEN

PRACTICAL STREET THROWING TECHNIQUES

Headlock Sweep / Harai Goshi

In a sacrifice throw, you first break your attacker's balance to his front or side corner, then perform a Harai Goshi (Hip Sweep). Next, you release your right grip and twist to the left, wrapping his head in your armpit and bi-ceps so that his body wraps around yours. Finally, you fall slightly to the ground and take him with you as you throw

your attacker. There will be occasions when you have no choice but to seize your assailant's sleeve, cheekbone, or jawline.

Shoulder Arm Grip

The Shoulder Arm Grip throw is a hand-and-leg technique. It is executed by grasping the attacker's shoulder blade on the same side and then spinning as if to bring them onto your side of your body while performing a foot sweep to throw them down.

The person executing this technique uses both hands to grip the attacker's shoulder blade and sleeve. Grabbing any clothing will work.

The critical points of this technique are as follows: Normally, the person performing this technique engages the attacker's shoulder blade area by grabbing some clothing or grabbing a chunk of skin if there is no clothing.

One Arm Shoulder / Ippon-Seoi-Nage

The basic principle of seoinage arm shoulder throw is to load the attacker onto your back and throw them over your shoulder in a forward direction. This particular technique is an excellent self-defense move,

When someone grabs you from behind, you grab their arm and bow forward. The person holding you usually does not think that the person they are grabbing would be able to do something of this nature.

The key to the technique in this book is to look at the picture with detail in mind. Think with the idea that a photo can speak a thousand words. Think about explaining a technique with no pictures, just how difficult it would be to learn and develop the skill of self-defense.

Circle Sacrifice / Kazuri Tomoe Nage

The **Tomoe-nage (Circular throw)** technique submarines under the attacker and throws them with a leg throw.

From the natural posture, the person executing a defensive technique waits until the attacker makes a lateral move. At that moment, the person conducting a defensive strategy bends their knee and places a foot into the attacker's abdominal area, then kicks off, launching a backward roll with his body curled into a tight ball and submarines beneath the attacker.

The springing Force of his bent knee to throw the attacker by kicking upward toward an arcing or sideways motion will complete the defense.

The person executing this technique uses his lifting hand and pulling hand with a kicking force.

Kibisu-Gaeshi

In the Kibisu-gaeshi **(One-hand drop)** technique, the defender grabs one of the attacker's advancing legs with one arm and tackles him onto his back.

With his right hand pushing at the chest area, firmly gripping the attacker's left leg, The person executing the technique then pushes the attacker down onto their back.

Outer Sweeping / O-Soto Gari

The person executing **Outer Sweeping / O-Soto Gari,** a technique that grasps the attacker's collarbone area to pull the attacker forward easily. Next, the defender grabs the attacker's sleeve just below the attacker's elbow.

The person executing the defensive technique pulls the attacker toward the person performing a technical side while moving forward toward the attacker and extending his Support leg to the outer side of the attacker. At the same time, the person executing a technique bends the knee of his side leg and prepares to move behind the attacker. Pulling the attacker's body snugly against his own, the person executing a defensive technique tilts the attacker's center of gravity to one side and then performs the reap.

When the attacker's center of gravity tilts, the person executing a technique swings his reaping leg around the attacker's body-weight supporting leg and reaps it in a sudden back-to-front motion. The reaped leg swings out behind the person executing a technique; by continuing to swing the leg upward until the bottom of the foot faces the ceiling, the person is conducting an effective Osoto-gari (Large outer reap) technique without losing power.

Sweeping Leg / Hari-Goshi

The defender begins with the person grasping the attacker near his collarbone and his pulling hand, holding the attacker near his elbow.

While lifting his pulling hand, the defender executes the technique, steps toward the attacker, and spins around, pulling the attacker against his back and side.

The defender executing this technique sweeps the attacker's feet from under them at the knee-to-thigh area.

Although the person executing this technique has only a one-legged stance, after bringing the attacker onto his leg and hip, he can throw the attacker by swiveling his hips and sweeping the attacker's feet and hips out from under him in a sudden explosive motion.

Both men and women use the **Harai-Goshi (Hip sweep)** technique without regard to rank, which can frequently be seen in competitions. **Hari-Goshi** is an often-used technique in the tournament world. Lightweight combatants rely on speed to execute this technique, and heavier combatants rely on power.

Deep Hip Wheel / Koshi-Guruma

To execute a **Deep Hip Wheel /Koshi-Guruma,** the defender begins by grabbing around the attacker's Head, similar to executing a headlock. Next, the defender grasps the attacker's mid-sleeve or wrist area with his pulling hand and the back of the attacker's collar or Head.

The defender executing this technique uses his pulling hand to pull the attacker forward while shifting his posture towards his left side, where his arm is around the attacker's neck. When pulled forward by the person executing the **Deep Hip Wheel,** the attacker's body moves toward the person performing the technique, thus inducing him to step forward in a circular motion.

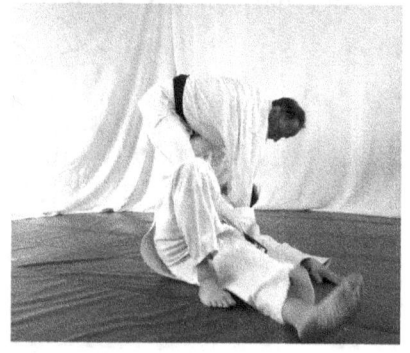

At this point, the attacker is in a sideways posture. As the person executing the **Deep Hip Wheel,** he swiftly turns his hip against the attacker. The person conducting this technique does this while bending his knees and bowing his upper body forward, destabilizing the attacker's balance toward the front and side.

The defender then uses the springing Force generated by straightening his knees and the Force of his arm around the attacker's neck to throw the attacker over his hips. This is accomplished by pushing his hips deep to the right, which causes the attacker's hips to be crossed by the defender's hips.

Two-Hand Reap / Morote-Gari

The Morote-gari is a two-handed reap that differs from the Kuchiki-taoshi one-hand drop. The Kibisu-gaeshi feel trip in that those techniques reap only one leg. In contrast, the Morote-gari two-hands reap reaps both legs.

Although the method of attack is similar, the Kuchiki-taoshi one-hand drop goes for the calf in all these techniques. The Kibisu-gaeshi heel trip goes for the heel to destabilize the attacker toward his rear. Still, the Morote-gari two-hands reap grabs the attacker's legs and tackles him onto his back. This technique is performed when the attacker relaxes his guard, requiring a swift, coordinated movement.

Outer Leg Block

The defender concedes by giving up one level of elevation as a sacrifice. After stepping deeply between the attacker's knees with either his left or right leg, the defender will use one of his legs to catch the attacker's left leg while wrapping it with his left arm from the outside. The defender will then fall forward with a twist to fling the attacker to his side and backward, and the defender will finish the move by kicking the attacker in the back.

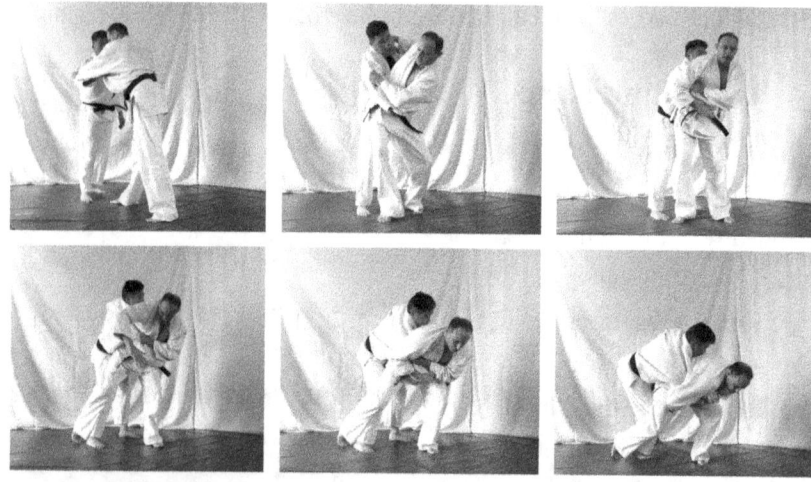

Hip Wheel / Koshi-Guruma

The person defending themselves will begin by gripping the back of the attacker's collar with one hand and the place in the middle of the attacker's arm where he is pulling with the other hand. The individual using this method uses the tugging hand to draw the attacker forward while simultaneously moving the hand on the back of the attacker's collar into a position around the attacker's neck.

When pulled forward by the person executing this technique, the attacker's body moves toward the person who draws their hand, thus inducing him to step forward.

The assailant has assumed a sideways posture at this point in the fight. The person using a method will quickly swivel around and press their hip against the aggressor as they put their arm around the neck of the person attacking them. The practitioner of this method does so while bending his knees and bowing forward, which throws off the attacker's equilibrium as he moves toward the front of the room. The person using this technique will generate a spring force by straightening his knees and then combining that Force with the Force of his arm around the assailant's neck to fling the attacker over his hips and onto the ground. This is accomplished by pushing his hips deep so that they are crossways to the attacker's hips.

Large Outer Reap / Osoto-Gari

When utilizing this technique, you rapidly grab the area around the attacker's collarbone or neck and pull it forward toward your shoulder area or chest. This defensive maneuver is carried out by the defender pulling in such a way as to sway the attacker's balance. At the same time, the defender moves toward the attacker and extends his support leg to the attacker's outer side.

At that exact moment, the defender will flex the knee of the leg to

his side and get ready to maneuver behind the aggressor. By drawing the attacker's body close to your own and shifting the attacker's center of gravity to one side, the other leg will raise, transferring the weight of the attacker's body on the leg the defender is reaping.

When the attacker's center of gravity shifts, the defender who is using this defensive method reaps the attacker's body weight by sweeping his reaping leg around the attacker's supporting leg for body weight and then reaping it in a rapid back-to-front motion, the reaped leg is swung out behind the person who is performing the technique. The O-Soto-gari is a technique that is both fundamental and symbolic of Judo.

Large outer Drop / Osoto-Otoshi

The defender executes a **Large Outer Reap / Osoto-Gari**. Implementing this technique, you quickly grasp the attacker's collarbone area or neck to pull the attacker forward toward your shoulder area. The defender conducting this technique pulls in such a manner as to sway the attacker toward themselves, executing a defensive technique while moving forward toward the attacker and extending his support leg to the outer side of the attacker.

At the same time, the person executing this technique bends the knee of his side leg and prepares to move behind the attacker.

Pulling the attacker's body snugly against yours, the person executing a defensive technique tilts the attacker's center of gravity to one side. Hence, the other leg lifts, shifting his body weight to the leg the defender executing a technique intends to reap. When the attacker's center of gravity tilts, the

defender executing this defensive technique sweeps his reaping leg around the attacker's body-weight supporting leg and reaps it in a sudden back-to-front motion.

The reaped leg swings out behind the person executing the technique; by continuing to swing the leg upward until the bottom of the foot faces the ceiling, the person executing the technique can complete a solid O-soto-gari technique without losing power.

The O-Soto-gari is both a fundamental and representative technique of Judo. Although it appears simple, it requires the proper execution of several fine points and is complex.

Outer Wraparound Throw / Makikomi

The defender executing this technique establishes a foundation by grasping the attacker's right arm near the shoulder joint.

Next, the defender executes the technique by stepping forward with his right leg, placing it outside the attacker's feet, then turning on the sole of his foot, setting his right foot against the attacker's shin.

The person executing the technique shifts his center of gravity slightly to his right leg, creating a dashing appearance to his stance. Next, his right leg bends toward the ground, then snugly holds the attacker's right arm. After grasping the attacker's right arm, the defender executing this technique twists to drive himself toward the ground. Then, the defender throws the attacker while sacrificing his posture.

CHAPTER SIXTEEN

JOINT BARS, CRANKS, AND LOCKS

Outward Wrist Lock

A wristlock is a type of joint lock that predominantly affects the wrist joint and, in certain situations, also affects the radioulnar joint, which is made up of two bones in your Forearm through hand rotation. When attempting to apply a wristlock, it is common practice to seize the hand of the opponent and then attempt to bend or twist it. The police also employ these holds to coerce people into surrender.

When someone tries to grab your lapel, you should grip their fist instead of their hand since this causes their fingers to become trapped in your clothing. At that point, twist toward the outside of their body; if they grab with their left hand, twist and turn toward their left, and vice versa. If they grip with their right hand, twist and turn toward their right.

As you twist and apply pressure to the opponent's wrist and elbow, turn the opponent's hand to face outward. There are around ten different holds. It would be best to pull with your fingers on the inside of your wrist while pushing your thumbs between the back knuckles. The joints lock more quickly when the elbow is 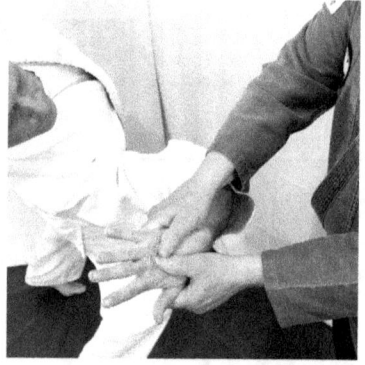 pressed against the torso. One hold modification involves twisting the wrist outward while forcing the opponent's elbow into the abdomen. To set up this variation, pull back, then drive forward as you attempt to throw off your opponent's balance.

Lapel Grab to Elbow Clamp Assist

The Elbow Clamp Assist is a standard grip that can be found in a variety of combat arts. The hold is administered to the opponent's hand

by bending it inside such that the wrist and elbow are bent to an angle of approximately 90 degrees. There are more than 19 ways to hold something, yet they all apply Force in the same way.

When using the hold, one hand pulls down and inward at the wrist toward your body, while the other hand bends the attacker's hand toward their body. When applying the hold, you can stand directly in front of the opponent or out to the side at about a 45-degree angle. Keep the gripped hand pointing toward the vertical midline of the opponent's body, regardless of where you stand or how much the opponent's arm is bent. This is important to remember, irrespective of where you stand. If the Force is directed appropriately, it is optional to grab something firmly. Plant the hand you are holding on your chest and use the weight of your body to achieve greater strength. Apply consistent pressure to the joint of his thumb by pressing the palm heel of your other hand against the joint at the very tip of his thumb. For example, push the heel of your left hand on the joint at the end of your thumb. While you draw his wrist away from you with the other hand, you should apply pressure to his thumb joint to compress it into his hand. This should be done while you pull with the other hand.

Tricep Grab

You end up with an arm bar when you defend with a tricep grasp. In an arm lock known as an arm bar, the arm is fully extended while the elbow joint is locked. Arm bars focus their attacks on the elbow, which can result in discomfort or even joint dislocation. However, other bars involve attacks on the shoulder and wrist. Arm bars, which are similar to Hapkido, typically involve more extensive usage of wrist locks and pressure points to assist in maintaining the grip. In keeping with this school of thought, HapJu-Kido incorporates many techniques that aim to throw the opponent off balance.

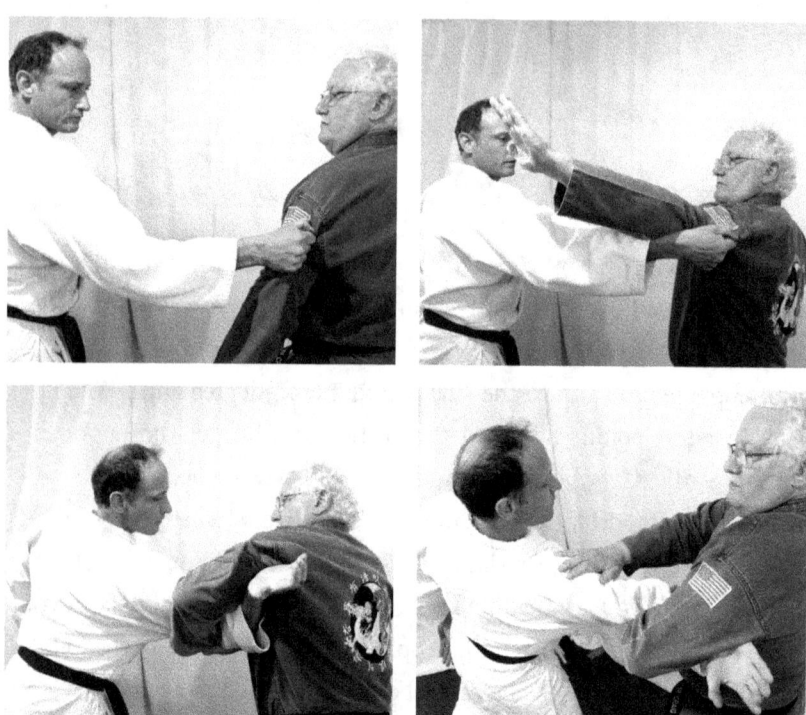

Chicken Hand Goose Neck / Hyperflexion Wrist Lock

A **hyperflexing wristlock** involves driving the wrist into hyperflexion by pushing or tugging the hand toward the inside of the Forearm. This type of wristlock is commonly referred to as a **gooseneck**. Conducting a hyperflexing wristlock in conjunction with a rotating wristlock is standard practice. This is because a hyper-flexed hand makes an excellent lever for twisting, improving the wristlock's overall effectiveness. Wristlocks that hyperflex the wrist allow for solid control and a progressive rise in pain if additional leverage is applied.

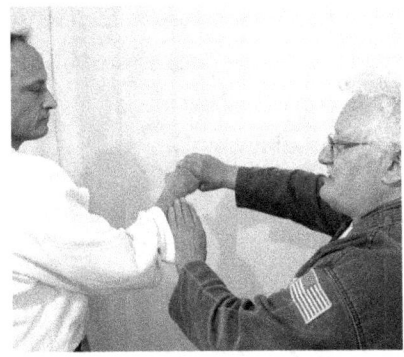

For this reason, hyperflexion wristlocks are frequently highlighted as a pain compliance technique. The hyper-flexing wristlock is another common type of wristlock applied as a submission hold. Hyperflexing wrist locks are a characteristic technique in **Tai Chi Ch'uan**. These locks are typically administered after an opponent **successfully escapes from a rotational wrist lock.**

Top of Shoulder Grab

After being given many warnings and having someone put their hands on you, you have the legal right to use any technique of self-defense that is proportional to the amount of assault that was committed against you. This right applies even though you were warned multiple times. This particular

move is a lightning-fast application of an armbar that incorporates a wrist lock and an elbow strick. The movement also uses the space created by the opponent's open guard. You can turn a blow on the elbow into an armbar by applying pressure and striking the elbow simultaneously.

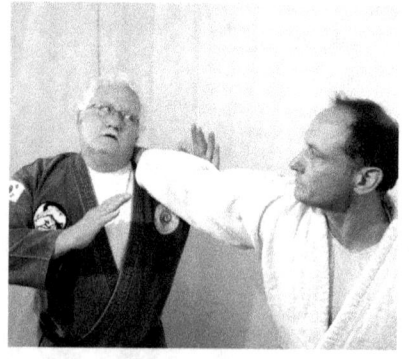 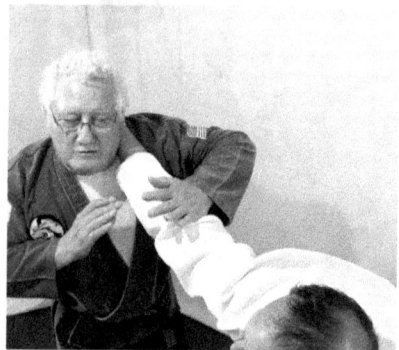

Side by Side, Huge

 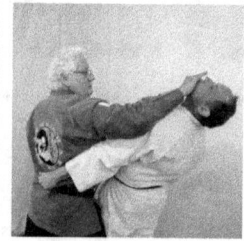

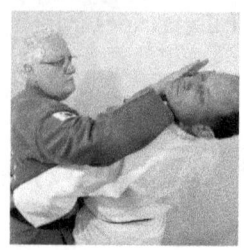 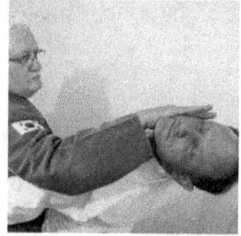

They are standing next to you and putting their arm around you. The concept behind this technique is that you should move swiftly while turning slightly toward the aggressor. Simultaneously, as the photo shows, you should place your palm under the person's chin and push at an angle.

The following stage in the execution of this technique consists of taking a small step behind the opponent and then tripping them as they attempt to take a step backward, which will most likely cause them to lose their balance and tumble.

They are in your face

The bottom of the jawline is quite close to the surface of the skull, so it's easy to exert pressure there if someone comes in your face. Below the jawline, soft tissue is present. Danger lurks in that area in every direction. They will instinctively flinch away in the other direction. The "fight or flight reaction " is a natural human phenomenon.

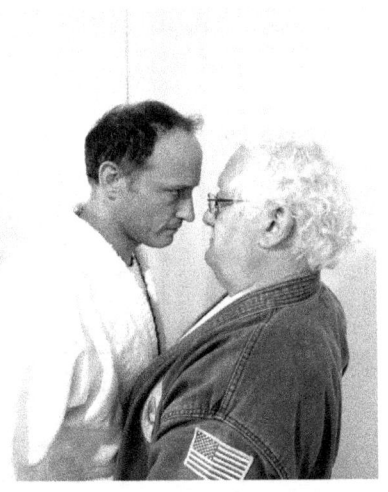

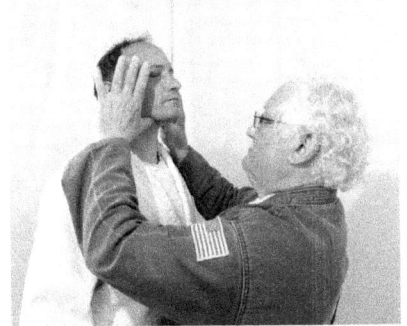

Goose Neck

The fingers are pointed up or down, and the wrist is bent forward. Keep your arm and body in contact with your opponent's bent elbow. Using one or both hands, press the palm against the forearm to lock the wrist. With the thumbs pressing against the inner wrist, place your fingers on the back of your hand. The gooseneck hold can be applied to bring an opponent to the ground or as an escorting maneuver.

Four Finger Hold

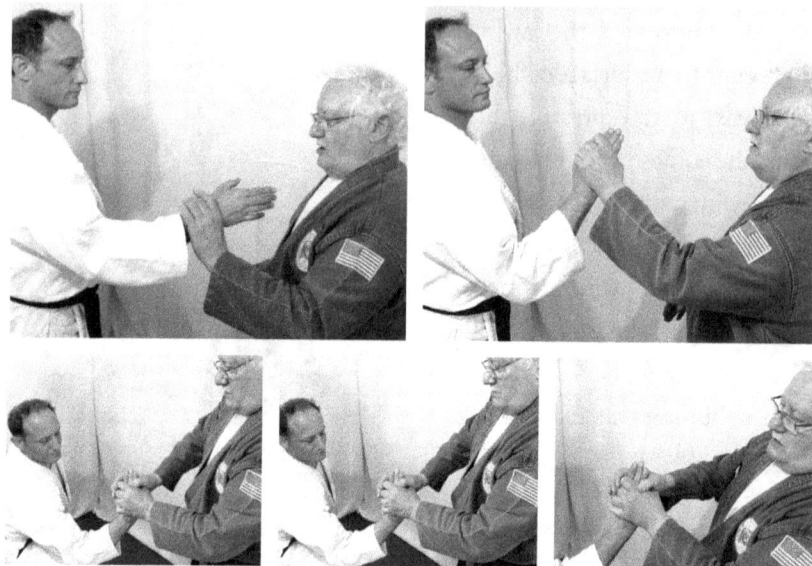

Many hand techniques in self-defense require particular skills and a lot of practice to develop accuracy. Practicing this skill set, you should find it easy to grab someone's finger and execute the wrist lock technique.

Because the joint needs to be positioned correctly to induce the desired level of discomfort, this technique is substantially more effective when the wrist is bent to the hand's sideways (pinky-side) position, which leverages toward the ulna side of the forearm.

Two-Hand Palm Press

Turn their hand so the palm faces outward while twisting and applying pressure to the person's wrist. There are around ten different holding methods. Nevertheless, the problem you are examining is the simplest one. When someone starts to lay their hands on you, it is common practice to apply this technique. Pull with your fingers at the inner wrist while you push with your thumbs in the space between the rear knuckles. The joints lock more quickly when the elbow is pressed against the body.

As you twist your wrist outward and forcibly drive your opponent's elbow into their stomach, a typical variation of this hold has you slamming your opponent's elbow into their gut.

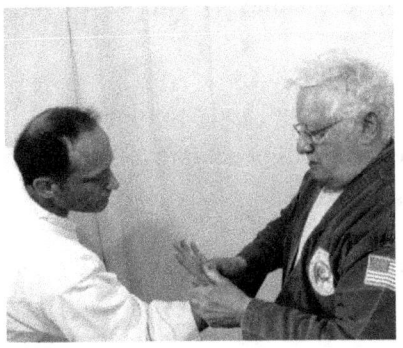
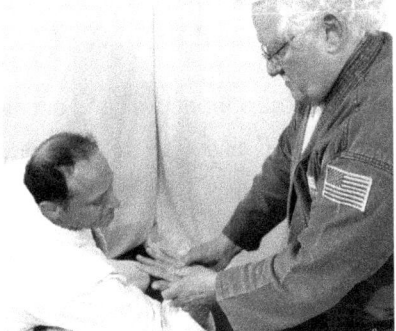

Boxing Thumb Lock

The thumb can be bent further than usual by pinching the thumb's tip toward the wrist's base. Put some weight on it by pressing down with the palm of your hand. Make use of your fingernails to pull.

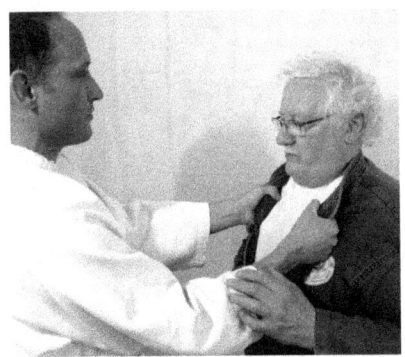
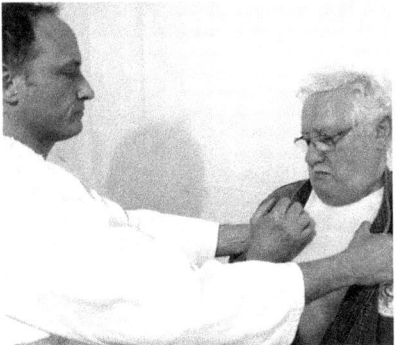

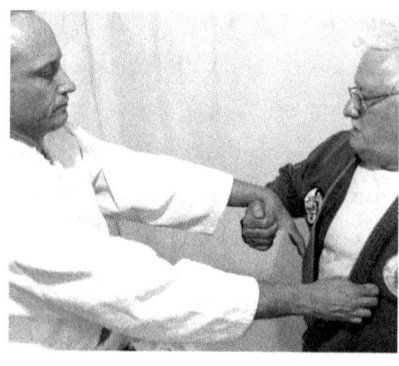 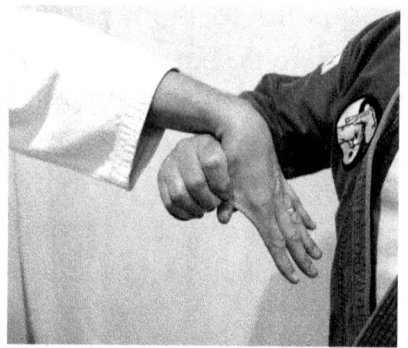

Outward Wrist Lock

Outward wrist lock works best by misleading the attacker of your intention to grab their hand.

Turn the opponent's hand outward as you twist and press down to lock the wrist and elbow. There are about ten methods of holding. All directing forces are similar.

Push with your thumbs or thumb between the back knuckles and your fingers at the inner wrist.

When the elbow is against the body, the joints lock faster. A common variation of this hold involves forcefully driving the opponent's elbow into the abdomen as you twist the wrist upward.

The most common method of applying an Outward Wrist Lock is with the opponent's elbow and wrist bent about 90*.

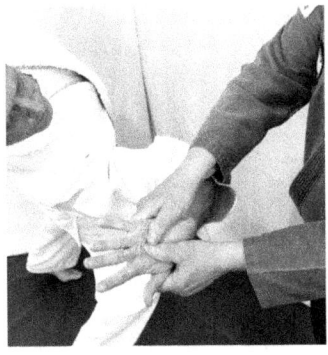

Another common variation is called a Pam Wrist Press straight down with your palm against the back of the opponent's knuckles

We can name a couple of other wrist locks: Scoop Wrist Lock, Elevated Wrist Lock, Front Wrist Lock, Scoop Palm Lock Side Wrist Lock, and Bent Arm Wrist Lock.

The point of mentioning the other techniques is to allow you to develop the most practical wrist lock.

CHAPTER SEVENTEEN

STRIKING POINTS ON THE BODY

General Target Areas

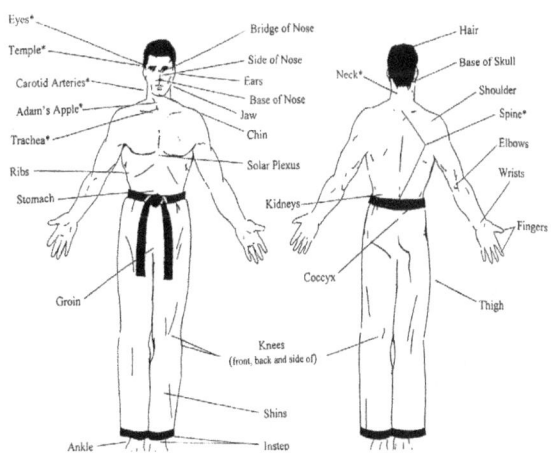

Temple / (extremely dangerous)

The method known as the four-knuckle strike should only be employed in the most dire situations, such as when another person's life is in jeopardy. The Bear Hand attack consisted of striking a large area with the palm in its entirety. With this, you can push in a straight line or make a circular sweeping motion. This blow resembles how a bear uses its claws, combining striking and tearing in a single motion. It is expelled from the hand by flexing the fingers and pressing them against the palm, then tightening the surface by expanding the palm and bringing the fingers closer together. The face, particularly the eyes and the ears, is virtually always the target of attention. After the initial hit has been delivered, the fingers can be used to grab the victim's skin or clothing or tear at them. The palm heal strike is easy to perform and will most likely end in the attacker getting a head ace as their best possible outcome.

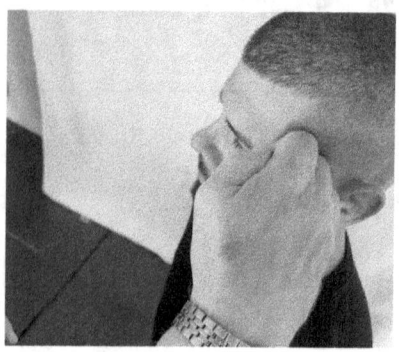 

Bridge of Nose

The hammer fist strike is usually only most effective in a downward strike. So, your targets are the nose, collarbone, side of the elbow, jawline, knee cap, and side of the neck.

There are three Hammer fist hand formations. In all three versions, the hitting surface is the bottom fleshy part of the hand. The picture to your left is the most used version of the three. The third version is called the Ki Hammer fist, but the picture is not shown. However, your index finger and middle finger are loose, similar to the picture of the knife hand, which allows for speed. The Ki Hammer fist is used widely in HapJu-Kido.

The knife-hand strike uses the snapping force of the shoulder and the elbow when it twists over at the last second.

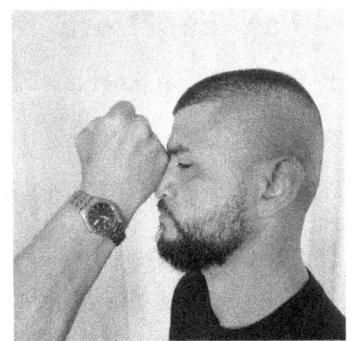

The knife-hand strike has three variations: the inside, the outside, and the downward strike.

Knife-handKnife hand strikes are executed using the same delivery motion as the Hammer Fist, using either the lead or rear hand. Striking areas include the temple, neck, back of the skull, and side of the torso.

The index knuckle punch is functional but needs to be more challenging to utilize correctly. It helps deliver a powerful strike into a confined space. However, extensive hand conditioning is required to build the finger strength necessary for the task.

The nipple, the space between the ribs, the temple, the neck, and virtually all areas of soft tissue are the primary targets.

The formation is a fore fist with the second knuckle of the middle finger extended. Bend the wrist slightly backward so that the knuckle is protruding forward.

Ear / Ear Drum

The palm-hand strike is exceptionally effective. It causes a tremendous ear ace and head ace.

A variation of the palm-hand strike is the old-fashioned slap.

The Open Hand strike, also called palm strike, uses the entire palm to strike a broad area. The hand may be formed in one of two ways: (1) by extending the fingers and stretching the palm to tighten the striking surface or by extending the fingers and cupping the pam.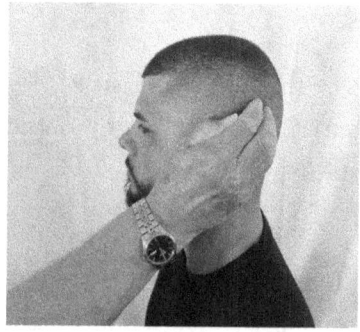

Targets include the tip of the nose, the side of the jaw, the ear, and the groin. Executing the palm strike to the groin is to distract the attacker so you can throw them.

> **Special note:**
> The KI is believed to collect in the center of the palm, which is one of the points where some people believe it enters and exits the body.

In martial arts, open-hand strikes can project destructive Ki into the target on impact.

Auricular Nerve Below Ear Drum

The thumb hand is a circular strike intended for targeted, precise attacks on especially sensitive or susceptible areas. With the thumb bent, locked, or rigidly stretched, make a relaxed fist and use your fingertip to stroke your eyes, neck, nerves, acupoints, or other soft spots. The strike can be delivered in any way, but the most potent way is to strike from the fist to the tip of the thumb, as seen in the image.

The Thumb Hand is one of the most decisive finger-spearing strikes because it can sustain an impact without suffering harm, unlike other finger-spearing strikes such as Spear Hands or the Five Fingertip Hand.

Nerve at Upper Lip / Base of Nose

This particular location on the body is susceptible to extreme pain.

This blow combines both hitting and tearing in a single motion, similar to how a bear uses its claws for the hand by bending and pressing the fingertips inward against the palm, stretching the palm to tighten the surface.

The target is usually the face, eyes, and ears. After striking, the finger can be used to grab or tear skin and clothing.

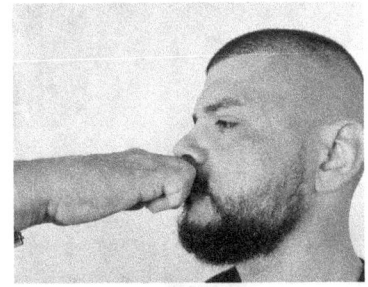

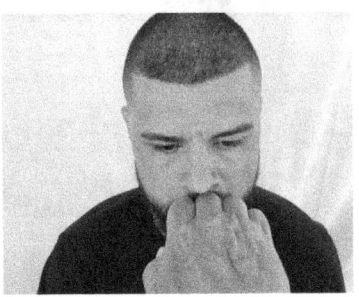

Tip of Jaw / Jaw

The straight punch is a thrusting strike in which all power is focused on hitting through a target directly ahead. The punching hand follows a straight line.

To intensify the punch, a twisting motion focused power and may produce a cutting effect on the facet targets. The strike is executed with either hand from any stance while stationary or moving in any direction. Punching power depends on your speed and the twisting motion of your hips.

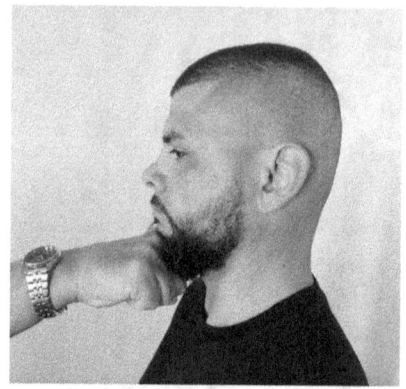

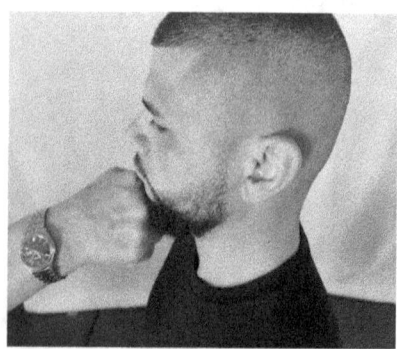

An excellent old-fashioned front kick can do the trick if you are quick enough to distract your attacker.

Cheek Bone / Chin / Cheek

The straight punch is a thrusting strike in which all power is focused on hitting through a target directly ahead. The punching hand follows a straight line.

To intensify the punch, a twisting motion will intensify the strike and may produce a cutting effect on the facet targets. The strike is executed with either hand from any stance while stationary or moving in any direction. Punching power depends on your speed and the twisting motion of your hips.

Adam's Apple Larynx / Extremely Dangerous / Trachea

Attacking the Adam's Apple is a simple task. You can defend yourself with your hands using a variety of tactics, such as the knife hand, forearm, middle knuckle, and four-knuckle technique, as demonstrated in the photographs.

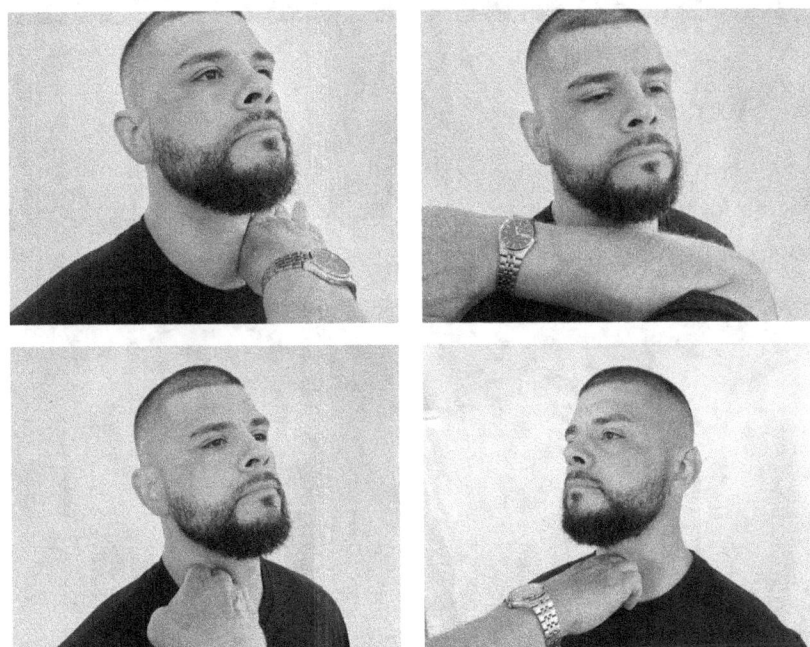

Collarbone (clavicle) / next to the trachea

Until now, every illustration in this book has shown how beneficial it is to use basic, uncomplicated attacks as self-defense.

> **Note:**
> It is pretty simple and suitable to use these basic hand methods to assault an assailant whenever they get control of you.

Stomach

It is typical for casual onlookers to overlook the benefits of hitting slightly lower, into the stomach. A slightly tilted approach is best for kicking someone in the stomach.

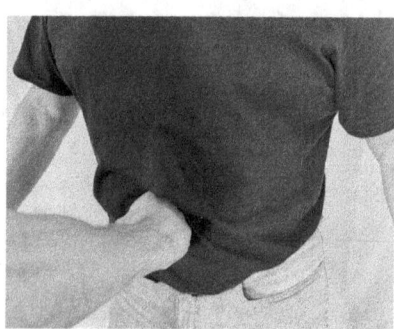 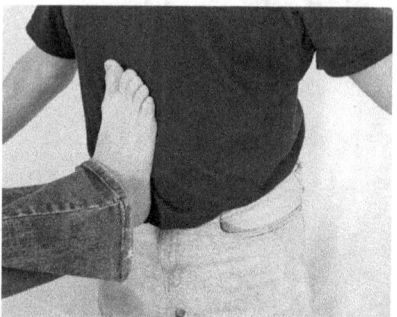

Striking below the belly button is the intended outcome.

Knees – Front, Side, Back, and Shins

This application is a terrific distraction and one of the most basic techniques for targeting someone's knees. In addition, they are quick to use and have a high damage output.

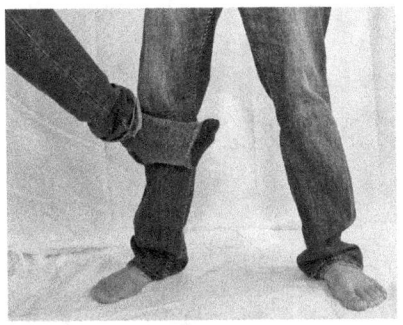
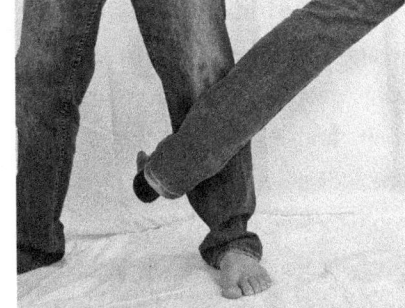

Solar Plexus

Punches to the Solar Plexus with the elbow, front fist, or forearm work well. Anyone within arm's reach can benefit from these three methods.

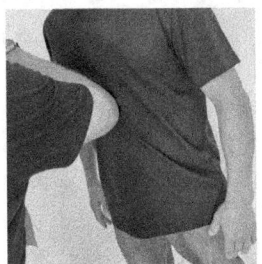
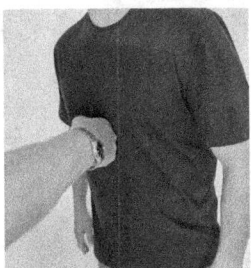

Ribs, Thoracic Nerves between Ribs

The ribs and the nerves between the thoracic ribs are extremely delicate tissues. The photographs below illustrate the most accessible body portion to assault this location: the Kobaton, the thumb point, the elbow, and the four knuckles. Observe the image with the crimson backdrop.

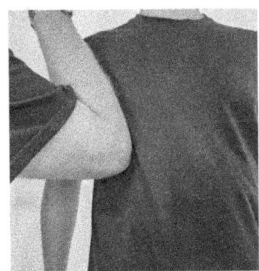
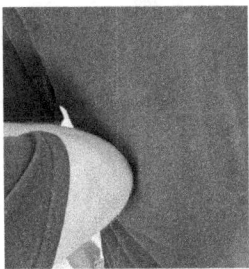
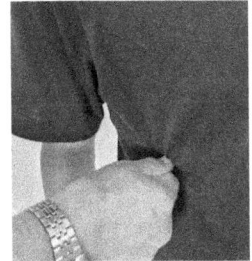

An illustration of the Kobaton weapon can be found here. It is what people use to carry around their house and car keys. The one displayed here is more sophisticated than the others from two decades ago. They lacked a gripping technique and were hefty. It would be easy to misinterpret this Kobaton as a weapon akin to brace knuckles.

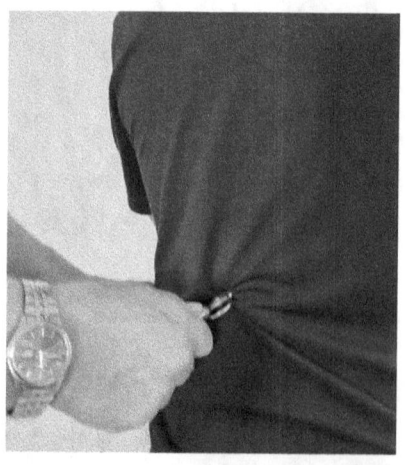

Noteworthy:
This weapon is the best tool for achieving pain compliance. Yes, we refer to it as a weapon as it may inflict severe, instantaneous harm on an assailant. You can use this device to deter an assailant and hit them repeatedly to ensure they won't attack you again, depending on the type of attack.

In Step / Ankle Joint

Simple stomping movement characterizes these two approaches.

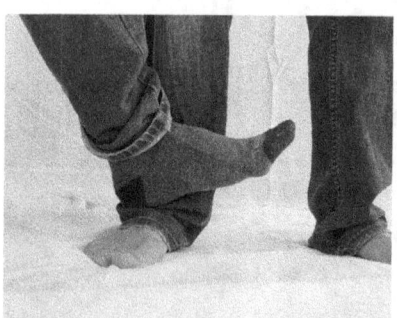
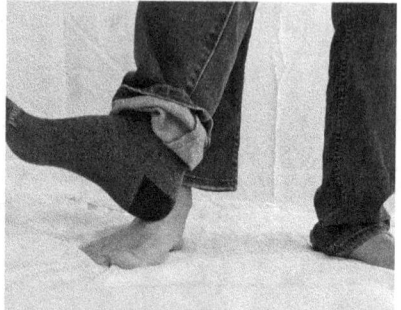

Practice with a friend is all that is required here. Keep your attention on repeatedly applying these two primary methods. It is acceptable to use these strategies more than once in real life. If you make a mistake, don't worry—you can keep stomping.

Hair

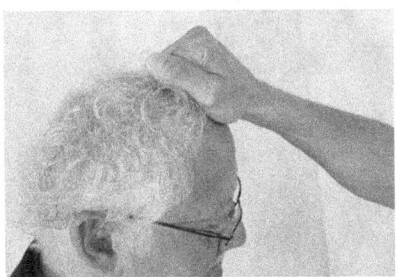

Let us be honest now. Here is the most straightforward method a human has ever devised. It is brilliant. Success is achievable by exerting a pull in any direction.

Base of Skull

A strike in these specific areas can quickly put a person to sleep. They are considered knock-out blows.

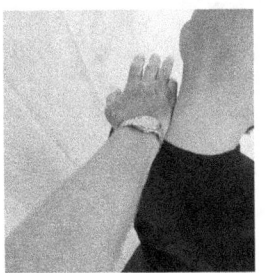 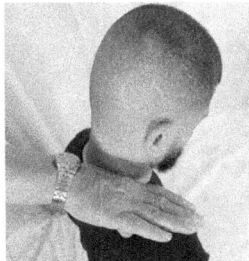 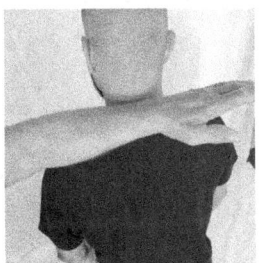

Looking at these three pictures is truly helpful regarding the striking location.

Shoulder and Shoulder Blade

When the scapula is struck close to the shoulder, it can cause much pain. It is, therefore, advisable to attack along the bone's edge when hitting this location.

Because there is dense connective white tissue along the edge of the scapula, this is the cause.

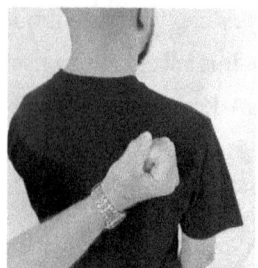 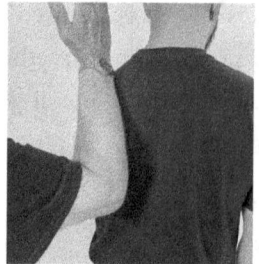 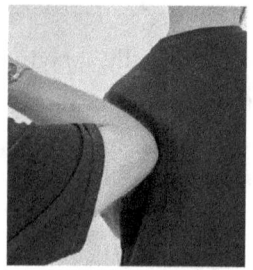

These two images show how to operate a Kobaton. You can carry your keys with this metal gadget called a Kobaton, a key chain. The defender (you) will wreak havoc if this gadget is used.

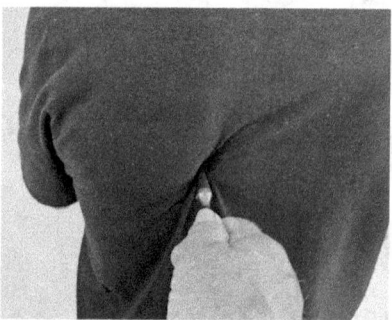 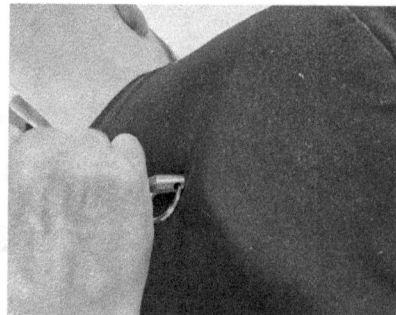

Depending on how much pressure you apply, every area where you push the Kobaton on your body will hurt.

So, it suffices to say that if you want to make a person regret that they attacked you, apply that degree of pressure. They for sure will be sorry.

An illustration of the Kobaton weapon can be found here. It's what people use to carry around their house and car keys. The one displayed here is more sophisticated than the others from two decades ago. They lacked a gripping technique and were hefty. It would be easy to misinterpret this Kobaton as a weapon akin to brace knuckles.

> **Noteworthy:**
> This weapon is the best tool for achieving pain compliance. Yes, we refer to it as a weapon as it may inflict severe, instantaneous harm on an assailant. You can use this device to deter an assailant and hit them repeatedly to ensure they won't attack you again, depending on the type of attack.

Elbows

Because the elbow's hardness permits powerful strikes, skilled fighters may effortlessly cut, knock out, or harm their opponent with a skillfully placed blow. An elbow works best when paired with punches or kicks. They are a helpful weapon since they don't break easily, but the range of elbow strikes is a drawback. Developing an elbow blow with maximum power takes practice and only functions well in close quarters. Fists are not superior to elbows.

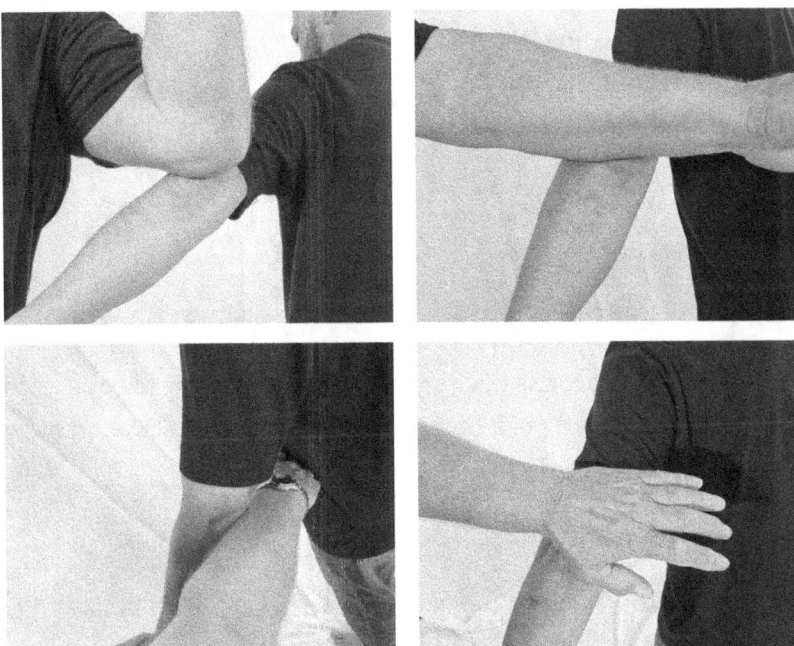

However, the reverse side of using an elbow is to attack the elbow with a forearm. A palm strike is pictured here to demonstrate the value of a close-quarter attack on the elbow rather than just discussing using the elbow as a weapon.

When the arm is straight, it is effortless to damage it.

Wrists

Applying basic tactics might easily cause someone to move away from you because of the intricate nature of the wrist.

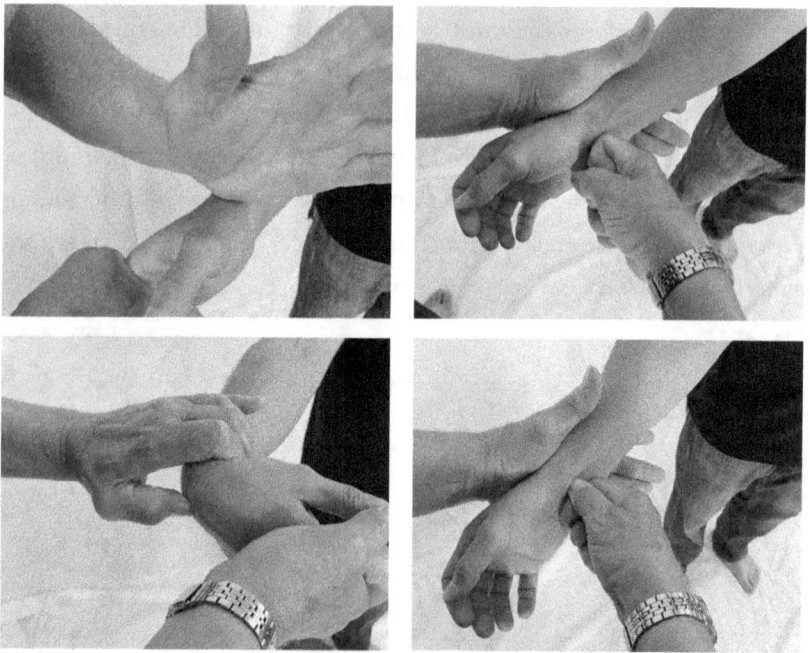

Practical tactics to use when someone is not expecting to be attacked in that way include the point of the thumb, a knife-hand strike, an index finger jab, and a bent wrist technique.

Fingers

The key to controlling the hand is holding onto the fingers in the pictures tightly. As you can see, it's easy to alter the direction.

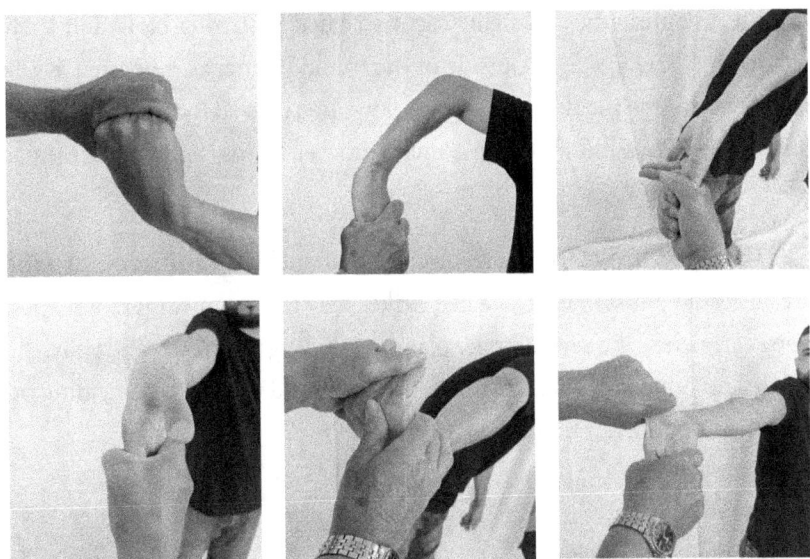

It is necessary to bend the fingers in an unnatural manner. A picture is worth a thousand words, as I have often stated. Grasping one, two, or three fingers is also crucial. You must know that doing so increases the likelihood of breaking a finger or tearing tendons or ligaments.

Thighs and Tailbone-Coccyx

The traditional strike to numerous body parts is the straight knee and shin. This brings us to the rear of the body, a roundhouse kick, as seen in the photographs, delivered straight to the target with a shin strike. A comparable attack is the penetrating or piercing knee. Penetrating the

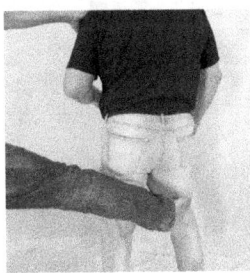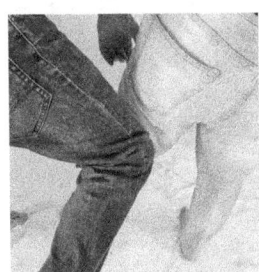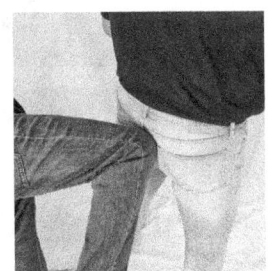

target with the rounded knee cap area still combines a hip thrust with the extension of the knee strike. The opponent's middle, which includes the ribs, diaphragm, and belly, can be struck with this blow and their quadriceps. The inside or outside of the rounded knee can be used as the hitting surface while delivering knee blows in a curved (outside-in, inside-out) manner. In addition to the stomach, curved knees can target the inner or outside of the legs.

The lower body striking techniques that enable closed-range striking are customary. Just like kicks, knee strikes may take many different shapes. They can also strike several other places, including the crotch and belly, the inside and outside of the legs, the upper body, and the head, depending on how their opponent's body is positioned.

Kidneys

An illustration of the Kobaton weapon can be found here. It's what people use to carry around their house and car keys. The one displayed here is more sophisticated than the others from two decades ago. They lacked a gripping technique and were hefty. It would be easy to misinterpret this Kobaton as a weapon akin to brace knuckles.

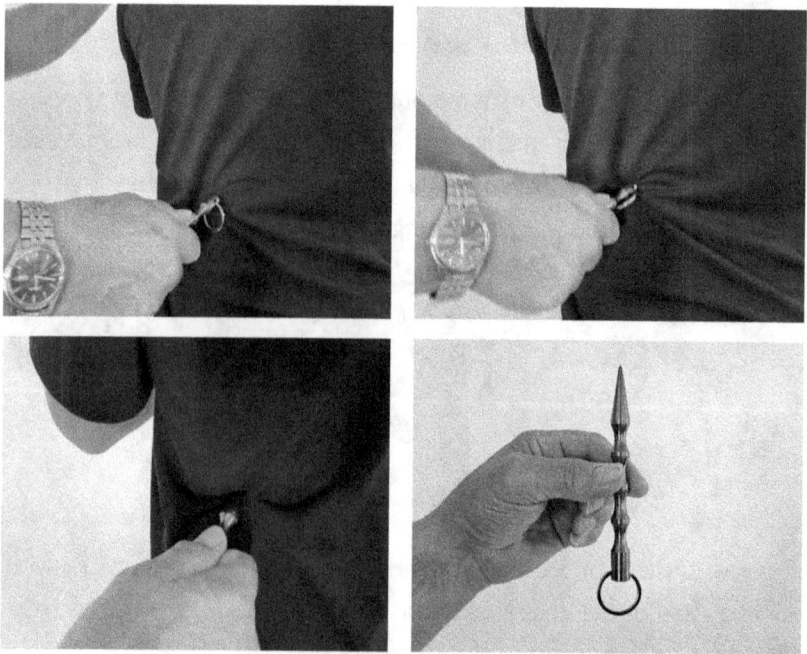

This weapon is the best tool for achieving pain compliance. Yes, we refer to it as a weapon as it may inflict severe, instantaneous harm on an assailant. You can use this device to deter an assailant and hit them repeatedly to ensure they won't attack you again, depending on the type of attack. I consider this weapon the great equalizer. If you want to encourage the attacker to leave you alone, I will enable you to use the blunt end where the keyring is installed on the Kobaton.

Neck

Instead of striking the spinal cord, pounding the neck merely aims to impact the primary vein in your neck artery carotid. One can pass out from a severe blow to this location. This is the sole rationale for targeting this region. Anything more would be a recipe for legal problems. Thus, be firm but also convey care.

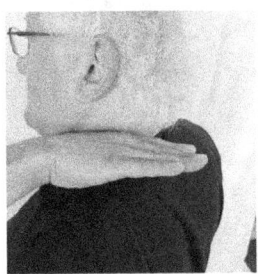 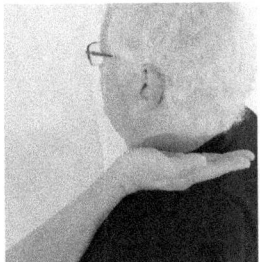 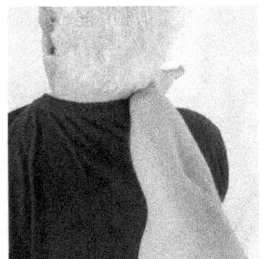

Back of Knee

A shallow depression at the rear of the knee joint is called the popliteal fossa, sometimes called the knee pit, compared to the cubital fossa. The tibia and femur are the bones of the popliteal fossa.

The knee's natural range of motion is 0–135 degrees, or from entirely straight (0°) to fully bent (135°). Hyperextension occurs when the knee extends past neutral by more than 10 degrees.

A hyperextended knee, also known as knee hyperextension, results from the knee joint bending incorrectly, which can harm the knee's ligaments.

Thick fascia spans the hip joint and continues downward toward the patella, tibia, and biceps femoris tendon.

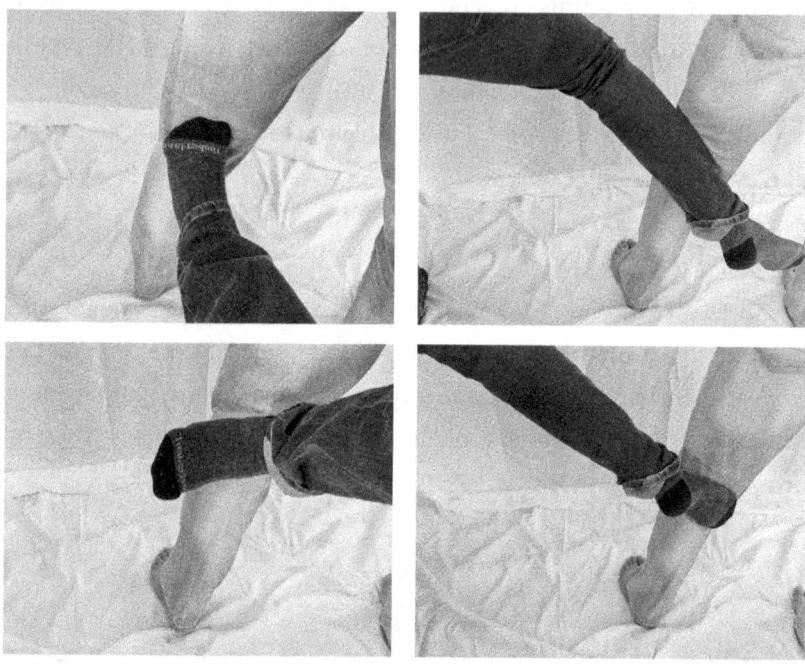

Sorry, this was my physical anatomy class kicking in. A kick to the side and back of the leg can cause much discomfort.

A strained knee, which affects the muscles and tendons, and a sprained knee, which affects the ligaments around the knee joint, are two separate forms of injuries referred to as "twisted knees." For clarity, injuries are typically referred to as twisted knees.

CHAPTER EIGHTEEN

UNORTHODOX STREET FIGHTING SKILLS

#1 Deflect /Headlock Take Down

Your opponent throws a Punch; you deflect with an open hand and then apply a headlock takedown.

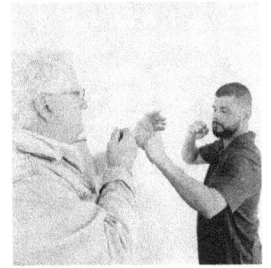 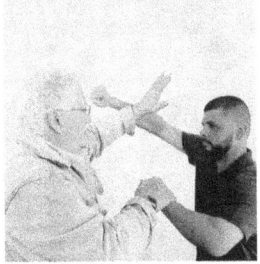 

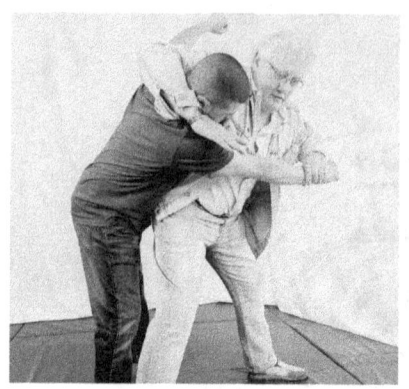
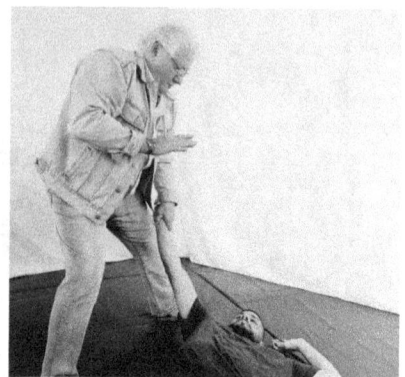

#2 Elbow Strike

You counter your opponent's jab with an open-hand deflection block, then hit them with an angular or horizontal chest or mid-section strike with an elbow.

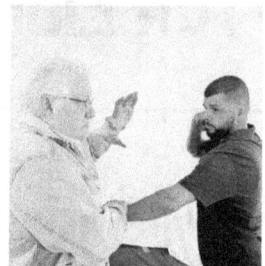

#3 Left Hand Jab

After deflecting the assailants' left jab attack, strike back with a right or left-hand jab.

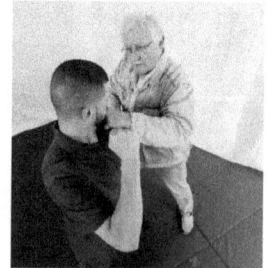

#4 Open Hand Flicker Strike

Pull the attacker's guard down; immediately execute a Flicker Open hand Raking action with a reverse claw.

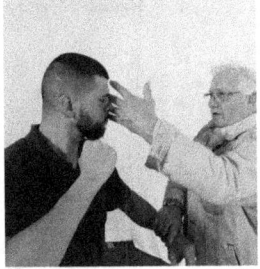
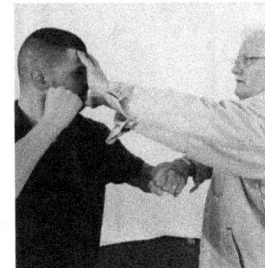

#5 Four Knuckle Upper Cut Punch

Using the hand closest to the attacker, take down their guard. Then, using the same hand to take down their guard, deliver four knuckle strikes in an upside-down strike.

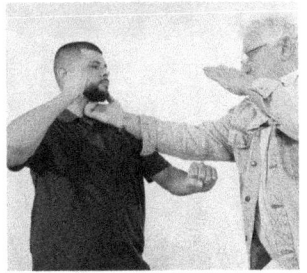

#6 Knee Strike

Take hold of the attacker's neck with one or both hands. Next, apply a knee blow to the pelvic bone or any other appropriate target.

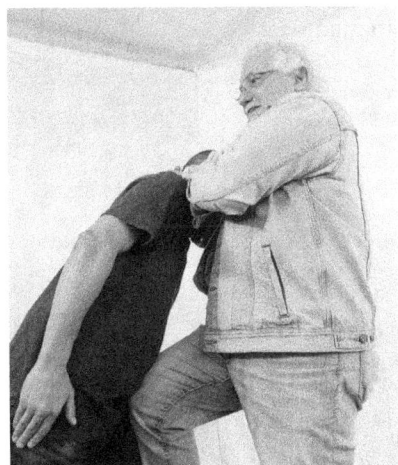

#7 Leg Sweep

Grasp the attacker's shoulder, neck, or shirt to defend oneself; tuck your head to deflect blows; disappear from their view; and use a sweep to force them to the ground.

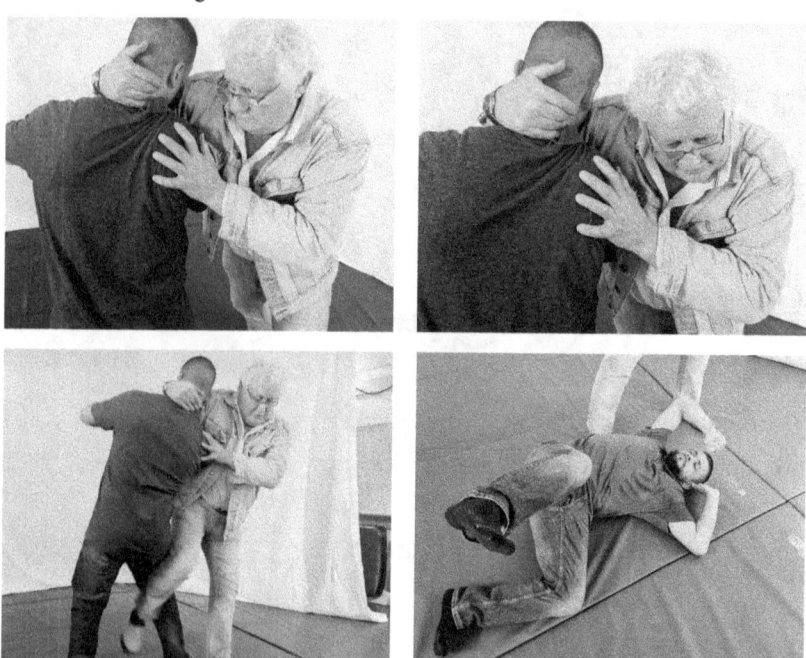

#8 Low Roundhouse executed with shine

Hit the assailant's leg from the inside or outside, and then deliver a jab simultaneously.

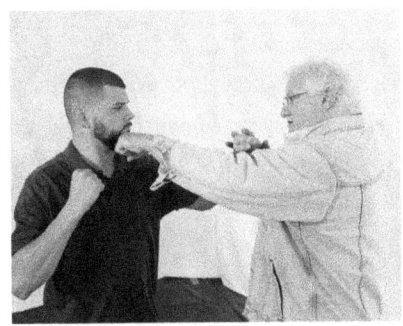 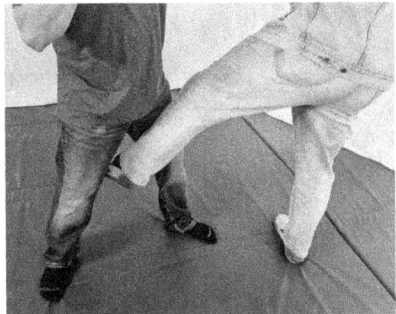

#9 Open Hand Flicker Back Hand

Immediately hit the assailant with a flicker live-hand strike to catch them off guard.

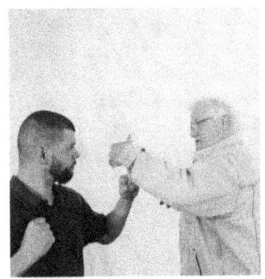 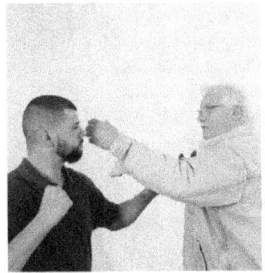 

#10 Ear Pop

Protect yourself by smacking the side of the head, especially the ear, with a cupped palm when the attacker is at arm's length.

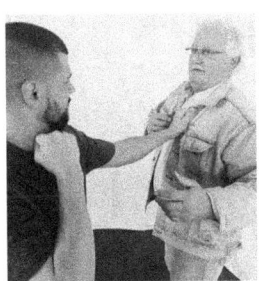 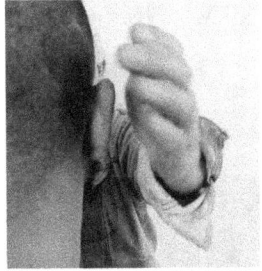 

#11 Pelvic Back Kick

Throw a back-kick toward the attacker's knee, pelvic bone, or thighs as soon as possible to surprise them by turning away and beginning to walk away. Here, the individual kicking is targeting the region of the pelvis.

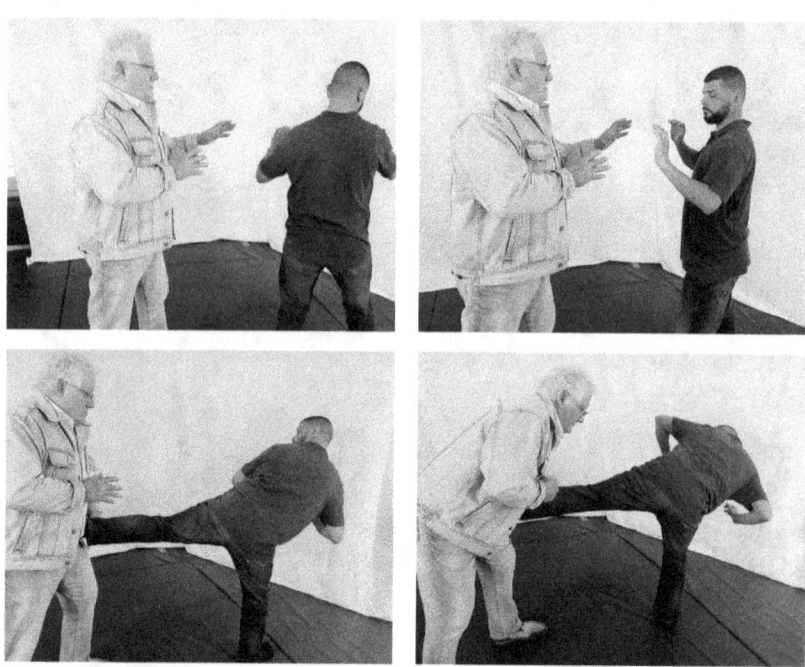

#12 Leg Grab

Leap toward the legs of your assailant and slam your body onto their legs. It is thought of as a Hail Mary technique.

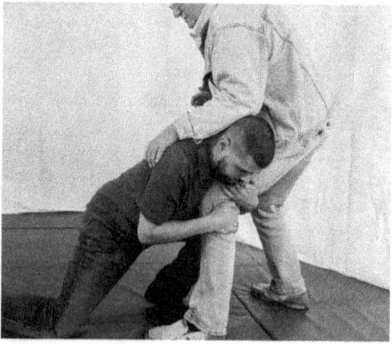

13 Forearm Thrust

Put your two forearms in an extended guard position, protecting your face. Subsequently, charge the assailant and strike him in the chest with both elbows.

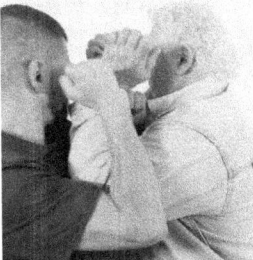
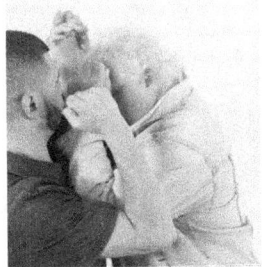

#14 Knee Clip

When you are behind the assailant, kick the back of his knees while grabbing his collar and pulling quickly downward.

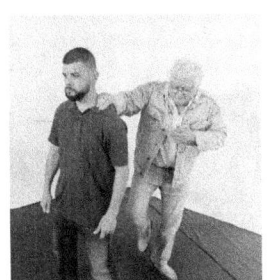
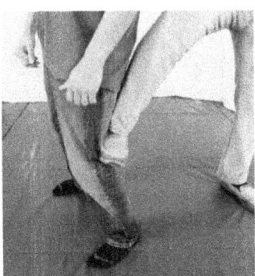
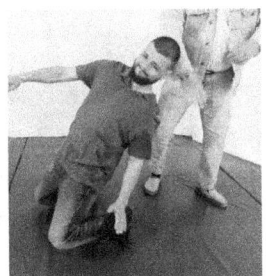

#15 Rear Naked Choke Hold

Apply a rear naked chokehold after you are behind the assailant.

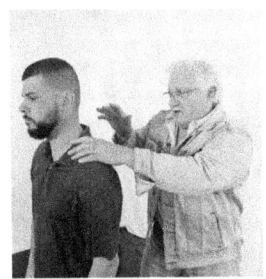
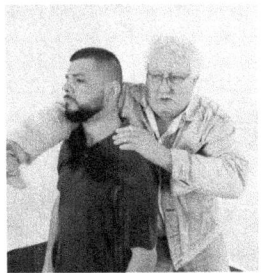
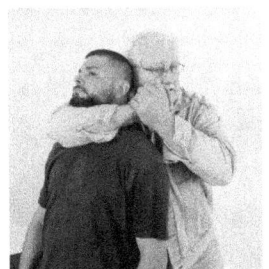

#16 Tuck and Role

Grab your attacker by embracing them from behind with a rear bear hug. The next step is to grab a leg and slither over to it. Then, fall in that leg's direction.

You can notice that in the second picture, my left hand is raised a little; I am attempting to change my grip but am taken down to the ground.

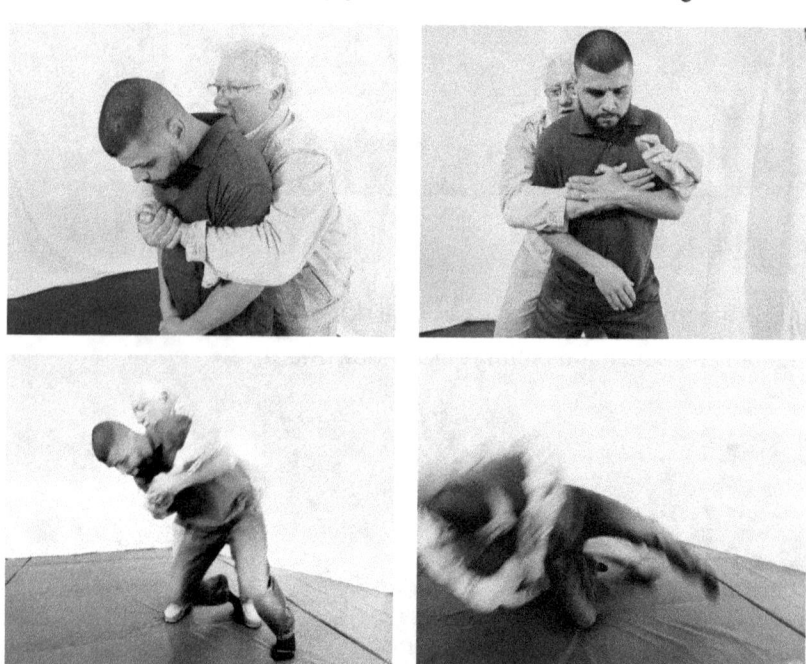

#17 Solar Plex Strike and Throw

Swiftly turn to face your attacker's side and execute a side elbow strike. Here, you slam your left elbow against his right side. You catch his leg by trampling on his left foot. Then, execute a floating hip throw. It is considered a sweeping hand technique or a hip throw.

  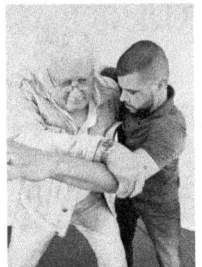 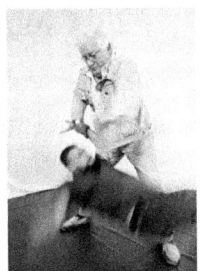

#18 Head Lock Wrench

When the moment presents itself, where you can execute a rear headlock, Place your side against his back and lean to your left, then throw him over or around your hip.

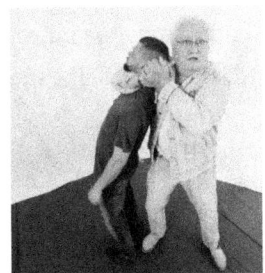 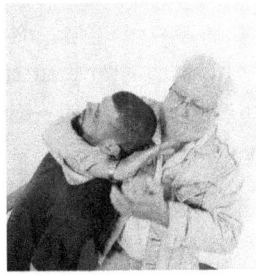 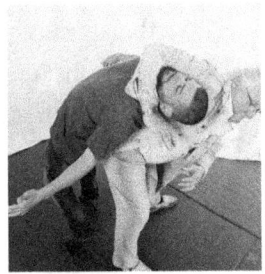

#19 Inner Knee Strike

Approach the assailant from the side and deliver a low roundhouse kick to the side or at a slight inclination of the knee.

#20 Club Kick to Backside

Leap forward and deliver a push kick to the attacker's rear at hip height while standing behind them.

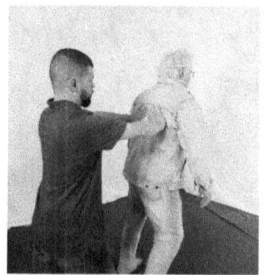
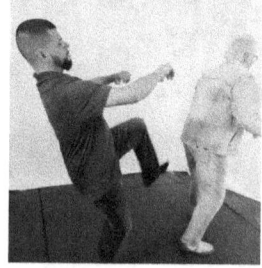

#21 Cross-Grip Strike

Take the attacker's arm by a cross-grip, using both hands to control his punch or grab. Support his arm with your right hand, then strike the attacker's elbow with your forearm. This will create a pinching of his elbow, causing much pain.

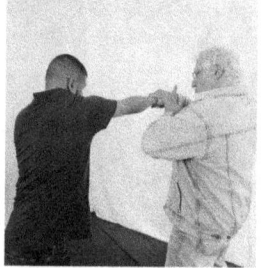
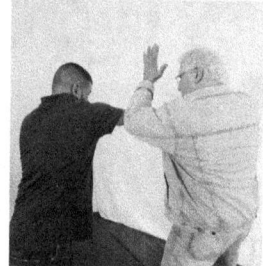

#22 Jugular Stike

Use the tip of your thumb to stab the attacker in the jugular vein. This strike is similar to doing a punch, but you are glancing at the attacker's kneck and connecting the tip of your thumb into the jugular vein. This attack should be done with caution.

Note:
this particular strike can be done very fast.
Minimal power is needed.

 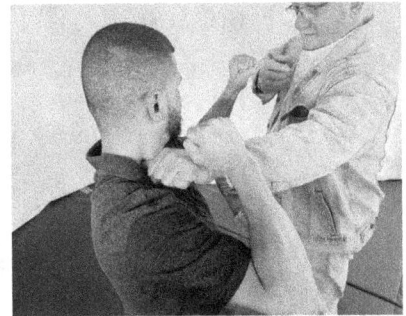

#23 Index Finger Poke

Poke the inside or outside corner of your attacker's eye with your index finger. Again, this technique is straightforward. The person will probably flinch because of the automatic response to protect themselves.

  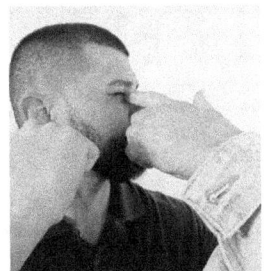

#24 Ridge hand Strike

Apply a ridge hand blow from behind to the side of the attacker's neck.

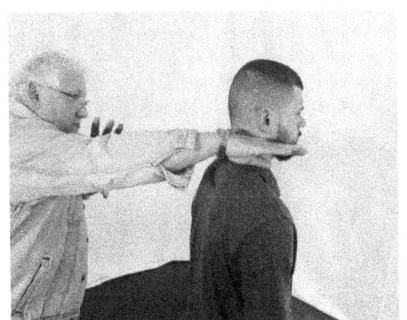 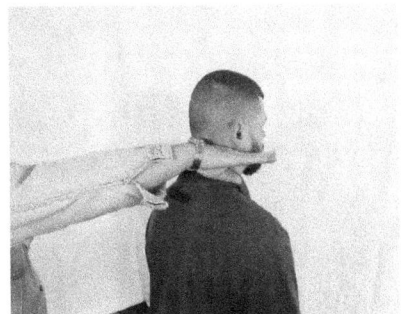

25 Hooking

While using your right leg for this technique, execute an inside leg hook to the attacker's right leg. Be very careful with this technique; you can quickly be taken down in the same way by your attacker by them doing a counter-leg hook.

CHAPTER NINETEEN

QUICK AND DIRTY

I refer to the Deadly D's as being Quick and Dirty in the classroom. Naturally, nevertheless, it would be preferable to avoid visiting the hospital.

The Internal Dialogue you hear in your head but have yet to teach yourself to listen to is called Quick and Dirty. It will shield you from the sounds that bullies generate when they want to scare you, in a sense. Your inner voice, which has been trained to disregard sounds and scream, will be able to defend itself. **The Deadly D's** are Deception, Distraction, Disruption, and Destruction.

- **Deception** is Nothing but a fancy word for lying. You must convince the bully that what you are about to do is a fact. The idea is to deceive him by verbally expressing the exact opposite of your actual intentions.

- **Distraction** is taking your bully's attention off you so you can reasonably catch him off-guard. The issue here is that it is only suitable for a split second.

- **Disruption** is a tactic or technique that messes with your opponent's plan of attack. Remember that it does not matter if he's an Emotional Hijacker or Bully; one thing is for sure: he sees in his mind that what he is about to do will succeed. So, dance around him so he gets confused about what he thinks he can do to you.

- **Destruction** is your physical ability to prevent him from hurting you; knowing where the vulnerable targets are, and the specific striking points to attack those targets will make you more effective.

HISTORY

The martial art of **HapJu-Kido** has developed and evolved over the past two decades. The fundamental components include Street Fighting, Tae Kwon Do, Hapkido, and Judo.

Techniques also used in Jujitsu, Korean Karate, boxing, wrestling, and traditional weaponry from Okinawa and the Philippines are incorporated into **HapJu-Kido**.

The art of **HapJu-Kido** is more than just a practical method of self-defense. Students of this kind of martial arts are encouraged to concentrate on improving all aspects of themselves, including their bodies, minds, and spirits. The martial art of **HapJu-Kido** teaches its students self-discipline, self-control, patience, perseverance, and respect for themselves and others. The instructors want their pupils to challenge themselves and try to advance in all facets of their lives, including the Dojang.

America's Historical Period

When did America's history start?

A question like "Where does the American story begin?" often defines America as an American nation. That nation, in turn, is typically described as starting with the 13 British colonies on the East Coast, the earliest of which was settled in 1607 (Virginia).

When was America named?

"**Waldseemüller** named the new lands "America" on his **1507 map** in recognition of Vespucci's understanding that a new continent had been uncovered following Columbus' and subsequent voyages in the **late 15th century**." Please note citations at the back of the book. In addition, there is a very informative website about who discovered America.

Korean history has six stages: the Choson Period, the Three Kingdoms Period, the Shilla Dynasty, the Koryo Period, the Yi Dynasty, and Modern Korea.

Choson Period dates to 2334 BC when, according to legend, the sky God Hwanin gave birth to Hwanung, who wished to descend from heaven and live in a world of humans.

During the Three Kingdoms Period, the Shilla Dynasty was founded in 57 BC, the Koguryo period was based in 37 BC, and the Paekchi Kingdom was founded in 18 BC.

The Shilla Dynasty (668 to 935) was known as the Unified Kingdoms period.

The Koryo Period was the Period from which Korea's English name was derived.

The YI. The dynasty lasted from 1392 until 1910.

In Modern Korea, Japan occupied Korea from 1910 to 1945.

"Japan surrendered on August 15, 1945, at the end of World War 2. In 1948, the UN established a democratic government in South Korea, with its capital in Seoul. Zoe Minjae."

Judo / Yudo

Korean Yudo was formalized during the Yi Dynasty and was thought to have been introduced to Japan during the Yimjin Conflict in 1592 AD; Japanese Jiu Jitsu, a general term that refers to a variety of different types of Japanese fighting styles, was influenced by early Korean Yudo (Judo) techniques as well as a variety of Chinese fighting systems.

Hapkido

Hapkido (the Way of Coordinated or Internal Energy) was founded by Choi Yong Sul (1904-1986). Choi was a native-born Korean. Hapkido is a complete martial art incorporating kicks, strikes, blocks, and deflections with joint locks, takedowns, and pain compliance or pressure point techniques.

Taekwondo

Taekwondo originated from the ancient Korean martial art of T'ae-Kyon, which emphasized powerful kicks. During the Silla dynasty, a military group called the HwarangDo was formed by King Chin-Hung, and they were known to practice this art.

CHAPTER TWENTY

MISCELLANEOUS TID BITS

Defensive posture is a skill developed by practicing bag work, shadowboxing, shadow kicking, and shadow throwing.

HapJu-Kido is a distinctly different martial art due to the infusion of street fighting skills. Beware, street fighters are notorious for unorthodox techniques.

Bag work and Shadow Training

You can improve your technique and physical fitness by spending rounds perfecting your technique on a heavy bag. This training style is used in all the different types of martial arts currently available. Shadowboxing is a beautiful way to practice each of the many boxing techniques and many other boxing techniques. You can evaluate the quality and precision of your technique by throwing various punches in front of a mirror or a large hanging bag. After doing so, you can make adjustments to your form as necessary.

There are three types of Judokas:

1. **Recreational** – practice for fitness and enjoyment

2. **Technical** – studies, Practices for self-defense purposes, and teaches most of their life

3. **Competitor** – Is only able to compete for a limited time, usually early in life

Craig Hutson has an innate capacity to convert his own life experiences into the ability to empathize with others. His father was an episodic alcoholic who had a near-fatal, horrific alcohol-related car accident that could have easily killed him and all five of his children. Craig's trauma from this event shaped the then eleven-year-old boy to be determined to be different from his father. Raised in a dysfunctional alcoholic home, Craig struggled to understand the rigidness and ineffective parenting that raised his sense of powerlessness. As an adult, Craig chose to form his understanding of what it meant to be a mature person by embarking on a journey in Martial Arts, which led him to develop a strong sense of emotional self-control.

Master Hutson's Bio

- Started martial arts at Kim's Black Belt Academy on Aug 13, 1973
- Aug 13th, 2023, celebrated his 50th anniversary
- Holds an 8th Degree in Taekwondo

- 7th Degree Head Master in KiMudo
- 6th Degree Senior Master in Kyukido
- 5th Degree Master in Hapkido
- 5th Degree Master in Judo
- Holds the designation of Expert Breaking Technician through Kyukido
- 2012, was inducted into the United States Martial Arts Hall of Fame
- Created BOMA – Brother Hood of Martial Artists
- Member in good standing World Kido Federation, Han Min Jok Hapkido Association
- United States Judo Association
- Received a Bachelor of Arts Degree in Applied Behavioral Sciences through National Louis University
- Vocational Specialist in Domestic Violence
- 1st Shaolin Temple Hall of Honors Award for Contribution to the Martial Arts
- Authored two books, *A Pathway to Emotional Sobriety and How to Get It*, and *Practical HapJu-Kido Practical Application of American Martial Art.*

Master Hutson's Five Principal Points of Self-Defense

1. Stay in the moment; be patient
2. Strike to Defend – Your Reality of the moment is your truth.
3. In each execution – hold Nothing back
4. Think your way into no mind, no self. Empty your mind, no fear
5. Only through ceaseless training can your techniques be concrete

DRAGON KIDO AMA of South Elgin is an elite martial arts school that focuses on providing one-on-one and semi-private instruction to its students. Students receive skilled instruction in martial arts from Black Belt Masters in the discipline of HapJu-Kido. This hybrid discipline masterfully merges the best parts of Korean Karate, Taekwon-Do, Judo, Hapkido, street fighter skills, and practical aspects of weaponry. Students also learn how to utilize various types of weapons. The HapJu-Kido curriculum that we follow routinely includes activities like sparring practice while wearing protective gear and competing in tournaments.

Our family-friendly martial arts school members have access to various popular programming options, including advanced black belt lectures, martial arts weapons workshops, and our Elite Academy Demo Team. In addition, training sessions that concentrate on either Judo or Hapkido as a form of self-defense are occasionally made available to participants.

Details regarding how to sign up for these specialized martial arts classes are usually shared in advance on our website dedicated to upcoming events. The HapJu-Kido Martial Arts Training program at Dragon Kido is operated solely based on reservations received.

Please email:
CRAIGHUTSON10@GMAIL.COM
if you want to be put on our waiting list and inquire about available appointment times.

In addition, we encourage you to use our multiple-session package options, which provide further savings, and to schedule your individualized martial arts sessions as soon as possible. The HapJu-Kido martial arts training program at Dragon Kido is only available to those with appointments. Email us if you are interested in being added to our waiting list and inquire about appointment availability. In addition, we encourage you to use our multiple-session package options, which provide further savings, and to schedule your individualized martial arts sessions as soon as possible.

The primary purpose of Judo is to develop a strong character. Budo in Kanji means warrior journey, but its main translation is "martial arts." There is a reason why the five stages were created: to mold a warrior with a strong character. The journey itself shapes a true warrior.

There are five stages to building a solid character.

Stage one, or the first level, is called Shoshin, and a beginner starts with the first kanji character. 初 Beginner, the second kanji, signifies heart. It can be interpreted as "beginner's heart" or "beginner's mind" when combining two characters. This calls for the curiosity and sincerity of a novice who is eager to learn. Discovering the purpose of your education is crucial since it will serve as the basis for your tenacity and drive.

The second level is called Zanshin. Kanji initially means to stick or stay. 初, the second kanji denotes the heart or mind. When combining two kanji, "lingering mind" is the usual translation. When you're on this stage, what happens? Despite your serenity, you have a high level of mental attentiveness. You are, therefore, conscious of your environment. Those with solid reflexes possess this. Similar to how instincts instantly tell your body to defend itself when someone is about to punch you. Therefore, you evade the enemy's blow or block it. Zanshin endows you with the ability to be vigilant and ready for any situation that may arise.

The third level is called Mushin, and it teaches you to control your thoughts and feelings so they don't influence your decisions or behavior. Combat tactics can be executed subconsciously by martial artists, enabling them to move with the freedom and speed of the wind.

The fourth stage, Fudoshin, represents the kanji characters "immovable mind" or "strong mind." An unwavering mind is the result of strong determination. Have you decided what your short- and long-term objectives are yet? How has it gone thus far?

Stage five, called Senshin, translates to "purified spirit." In life, there are some things we anticipate happening or accomplishing. These things become disappointments and dissatisfactions when they fall short of our expectations. You must let go of high hopes, accept the future with an open heart, live in the now, and face reality to achieve a pure spirit. That's the Senshin concept.

CITATIONS

- https://firephoenixmartialarts.wordpress.com/2015/07/17/the-three-principles-of-hapkido/
- Thomas Lickona, *Character Matters* (www.Amazon.com)
- https://thequiltedone.wordpress.com/2014/04/12/the-intellect-has-little-to-do-on-the-road-to-discovery/
- https://thequiltedone.wordpress.com/2014/04/12/the-intellect-has-little-to-do-on-the-road-to-discovery/
- https://inspiration.rightattitudes.com/topics/self-respect/
- https://www2.cortland.edu/dotAsset/299043.pdf
- https://www.dragonkido.com/
- https://www.judo-ch.jp/english/dictionary/technique/nage/te/ipponseoi/
- https://www.judo-ch.jp/english/dictionary/technique/nage/te/yamaarasi/
- http://www.turtlepress.com/training/hapkidos-danjun-breathing
- https://www.dragonkido.com/
- https://www.illinoislegalaid.org/legal-information/what-legal-definition-self-defense
- https://findanyanswer.com/why-is-virtue-important-in-life
- https://www.openpalmhapkido.com/health.html
- You Can Easily Judge the Character of a Man by How He Treats Those Who https://quoteinvestigator.com/2011/10/28/judge-character/
- https://cocot.vhfdental.com/did-amerigo-vespucci-encounter-natives
- https://en.wikipedia.org/wiki/Kick

www.ingramcontent.com/pod-product-compliance
Lightning Source LLC
Chambersburg PA
CBHW072210070526
44585CB00015B/1273